The Changing *Face of*
Manchester

THE CATHEDRAL

MH 39

THE BUS STATION AND GARDENS
PICCADILLY

A TUCK CARD

THE TOWN HALL ALBERT SQUARE

MANCHESTER

MARKET STREET

ST. ANN'S SQUARE

MARKET STREET.

PICCADILLY.

TOWN HALL ALBERT SQUARE.

MANCHESTER

SHIP CANAL, SALFORD DOCKS.

THE CATHEDRAL AND EXCHANGE STATION.

216758

The Changing *Face of* Manchester

Cliff Hayes

breedon **books**
PUBLISHING

First published in Great Britain in 2001 by
The Breedon Books Publishing Company Limited
Breedon House, 3 The Parker Centre,
Derby, DE21 4SZ.

08733147

Dedication

For Rose and Frank Gore,
who in their own gentle way care so much
about Manchester's history.

ISBN 1 85983 237 7

Printed and bound by Butler & Tanner, Frome,
Somerset, England.

Jacket printing by GreenShires, Leicester, England.

CONTENTS

ACKNOWLEDGEMENTS

Grateful thanks must go to Barry Armstrong, of Chadderton, for permission to use his photographs of Manchester in the 1990s. To Ged McCann for his *Manchester Today*, and to Gordon Coltas (Locofotas) for his steam railway photos. Special thanks must go to Ted Gray for his help and guidance, and for the use of his photograph collection. His knowledge of the history of the Manchester Ship Canal has been of great help too. Thanks to Alan Palmer for providing the map for chapter one, and to Arthur Haines and his wife Eileen (postcard and photograph dealers) for help finding some of the rarer views. Also special thanks to my wife Sylvia for typing and editing the manuscript.

PICCADILLY

CENTRAL LIBRARY AND CENOTAPH

THE ROYAL INFIRMARY

TOWN HALL

MANCHESTER

12 C

WHITWORTH PARK

INTRODUCTION

THE NAME Manchester is known all over the world. It was revered all over Europe in the early 1800s as the place where money was to be made as bargains were struck in the newly emerging cotton industry. It was a place where ideas were springing up, and where investors could cash in on developing schemes. In the 19th century it also became known as a place of refuge, and many European Jews found a safe haven from oppression here. The whole British Empire knew of Manchester as an exporter of cotton goods. Manchester cotton mills sent fine cotton goods all over the world. Sheets and bed linen with a 'Made in Lancashire' label were the best money could buy.

In the 1860s, during the American Civil War, Manchester was greatly affected by a shortage of raw cotton, but the area stood firmly behind the principle of the fight for freedom of the slaves. Many years later, in recognition of their support, a statue of Abraham Lincoln was sent to the people of Manchester.

The Quaker, Wesleyan and Methodist movements thrived in the city. These devout Christian free-thinkers contributed a great deal to the success and formation of Manchester. Quietly, they expounded their philanthropic ideals to help their fellow man. Manchester and Salford were among the first cities in the country to have night shelters, street missions, Sunday schools and libraries, and they led the world in implementing social and economical reforms which helped to change the lives and fortunes of citizens.

From a thriving area in 1800, to an area of poverty in 1860, and from an industrial heartland in 1830 to a dying city in 1870, the fortunes of Manchester have waxed and waned over the years. The building of the Manchester Ship Canal did much to revive the city's fortunes. Manchester liners sailed from the centre of Manchester to all points of the globe, taking Manchester's wares with them. Ships named the *Manchester Trader*, *Manchester City* and *Manchester Endeavour* could be seen in Canada, North and South America, and many parts of the British Empire.

At the beginning of the 20th century, Manchester was held up to the rest of the world as the success story of the Industrial Revolution. Smoke from the chimneys of Manchester meant money in the businessman's pocket, while thousands strived in the 'dark satanic mills'.

The book *Manchester Man* by Mrs Linneaus Banks sold millions of copies, and its insight into life in the city in the early 1800s spread Manchester's name wider. During World War Two, the industries in and around Manchester made it a prime target of the Luftwaffe and many areas were savaged by bombs.

In modern times the name Manchester is world renowned for sporting achievements. Football is the main reason for this, and Manchester United are known the world over, but the Lancashire county cricket ground at Old Trafford is an added attraction, and Test matches held there are watched all over the world. Technically both Old Traffords are in Stretford, not the city of Manchester, but most people associate them with Manchester. Manchester also hosts cycling, at the new Manchester Velodrome, and basket ball.

In 2002 Manchester hosts the Commonwealth Games, and people from all over the world will be welcomed to the city. Building the infrastructure needed for these games has brought many benefits, notably the regeneration of Gorton and East Manchester. The new 'Eastlands' stadium will be the home of Manchester City Football Club after the games. The olympic-size swimming pool on Oxford Road at All Saints is already greatly appreciated by Manchester residents, and will be an asset for many years to come.

Manchester is without doubt a great city that has grown to its present size through the power and activity of its citizens. The assertiveness that has made it great has also led to a desire to be at the forefront of change. This has led to a 'clear away the old' thinking, which has not always been for the best. However, the city is very much alive. New centres may spring up and grow, while others decline, but all the time the people and places of the city are interacting in a fascinating mix. The aim of this book is to capture this movement and vitality, and monitor the 'changing face of Manchester.'

Within the modern city of Manchester are many old 'townships' which were once self-governing. They are:

Ardwick	Harpurhey
Baguley	Heaton
Beswick	Hulme
Blakley	Manchester
Bradford	Moss Side
Cheetham	Newton (Heath)
Chorlton-on-Medlock	Northenden
Chorlton-cum-Hardy	Northenden Etchells
Crumpsall	Openshaw
Gorton	Rusholme

Manchester has lost Failsworth to Oldham, along with Denton, Haughton and Droylsden. Reddish and Heaton Norris were given to Stockport, and Salford claimed Broughton. Stretford was once part of Manchester, though the Trafford family held it under strict supervision. Salford too was once in the parish of Manchester.

OLD SHAMBLES

GRAND HOTEL

ST. PETER'S SQUARE

MANCHESTER

ST. ANN'S SQUARE

MHR.38

PICCADILLY GARDENS

Chapter One

THE FOUNDATIONS OF MANCHESTER

THE EARLY history of Manchester is defined by rivers. The city grew up where it is because of three rivers that run through the area, the Irwell, the Irk and the Medlock.

Manchester is situated within a large 'c'-shape, with the top being where the River Irk joins the Irwell. There was once a large red sandstone cliff at this point, and where the Medlock came to join at the inside bottom of the 'c' was another large outcrop.

Ancient man found these two positions and chose the high ground to the north for a settlement. This area, at the confluence of the Irk and Irwell, appealed because of its elevated position and closeness to the rivers. It also had a stream (Hanging Ditch) to the south of the headland, giving even more protection. This ditch was a rain and water run-

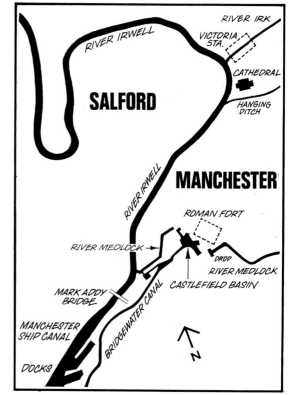

off from the higher area we now call Shude Hill. The southern outcrop had a large area of marshy ground between it and the River Medlock.

Over the years the ground now beneath much of Manchester city centre has been levelled off. Two thousand years ago the area where the cathedral is today was about 18ft higher. Other areas around Piccadilly Station and St Peter's Square are 10–15ft higher than they were even 300 years ago.

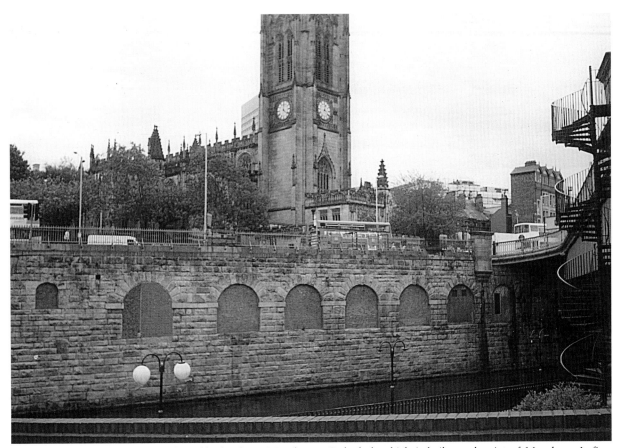

Looking across the Irwell from the Salford side to Manchester Cathedral, which is built on the site of Manchester's first settlement. Behind those bricked-in arches lies a Georgian street, under today's roadway. The Manchester side of the river is much higher than the Salford bank.

Two thousand years ago the rivers of Manchester would have been clear and sparkling, and the Irwell was noted for its eels. Until late Victorian times eel pie was a local delicacy. The River Mersey was a salmon river, and trout would have been found in all the local rivers. Oak, ash and yew trees are native to our area, and grew freely along the river banks, with hazel bushes providing much of the undergrowth. On the far side of the Irwell, willow trees grew. The latin name for willow is *salix*, and thus Salford is the ford where the *salix* grew. The name Irk means 'bounding rapid river'.

The ancient Britons who moved into the area are thought to have been the Brigantes, or at least a branch of that tribe known as the Cornavii. A bronze dagger from their time was found during excavations at Hanging Ditch. Behind the sandstone cliff was a breast-shaped hill, referred to as a *mamatory*. The first part of this word gives us the 'mam' which formed the name Mamucium, the city's earliest name. It later became Mamcester before being given its modern title.

The River Irwell is the major river of the area, though today we do not make enough of its calm and sedate journey through Manchester and Salford. Irwell means 'a vigorous winding stream' and it lives up to the name, proceeding almost snake-like through Salford before pulling itself to attention and passing Manchester in a straight line before reaching Old Trafford.

The River Medlock today could almost be considered Manchester's hidden river. From Ardwick and London Road it goes into a culvert and is piped as far as Princess Street. It then wanders past the back of the BBC building and under Oxford Road before re-entering a culvert and emerging just before Knott Mill.

Unfortunately the River Medlock has been used over the centuries as the drain and cesspool of Manchester. The river ran through many of the poorer areas where people had no alternative but to dump rubbish and slops into the river. Even today the river is full of shopping trolleys and plastic bags. The word Medlock means 'full lake' or 'damned area behind a weir', and the river did provide Manchester's early mills with their water power.

The River Medlock as it runs behind Whitworth Street and the former refuge building (now the Palace Hotel). The small archway is where Shooters Brook runs into the Medlock. (Barry Armstrong)

In the 1760s the river was so polluted that the Duke of Bridgewater was appalled that this river would provide water for his Bridgewater Canal when it finally reached Manchester. He gave his canal genius, James Brindley, instructions that water from the Medlock was only to be used in an emergency, and he solved the problem of keeping the River Medlock out of the Bridgewater at Castlefield in spectacular fashion.

When the River Medlock reaches the Castlefield area, it drops 16ft down a man-made well, then runs through a brick culvert under the Castlefield basin complex of the Bridgewater Canal to emerge 17ft lower than it was at Knott Mill. It then continues to join the River Irwell at Potato Wharf. This drop of one foot in water level means that gravity and its own momentum keep the water moving under Castlefield with no mechanical help. As the river passed under Castlefield it turned a paddle wheel which provided power for the lifts at the Grocers' Warehouse, built on the Bridgewater Quays.

Roman Manchester

When the Romans arrived in the Manchester area in around 79AD they needed a station, or stopping post, on the important route from Chester to York. Agricola, an area commander, decided that Mamucium was the place to build it. A wood and earthwork fortification was erected in around 80AD. The Romans chose the southern sandstone outcrop rather than the older, more northern, settlement. This may have been because it gave better views to the south and west, or because it gave extra protection with the marsh areas between it and the rivers, or simply because it was as yet undeveloped.

The River Medlock passes the winding gear which opens 'the drop' at Castlefield.

The Romans soon dug in at Mamucium and by 200AD the early wood and earthwork fortification had been replaced by a stone construction. There was by then a considerable town or 'vicus' growing up to the north of the fort, and this extended along the Roman road heading north to York, still within the safe enclosure of the local rivers. The Roman fort was roughly five acres in size and its centre was where the railway line from Knott Mill Station, heading north through Salford, goes under the Metrolink line from G-Mex. The area around the fort was inhabited by auxiliary workers, locals and others, and extended to almost three square miles. Artefacts from this 'village' have been found under Bridgewater Street and at Knott Mill. As the borders of the Roman empire were strengthened to the north by Hadrian's Wall and the Wall of Pius, Manchester (Mamucium) lost its frontier setting and settled down to become a distribution centre, a powerhouse behind the front lines. The non-Roman inhabitants would have been quite settled and protected by the community around them. In 1820, a well was found within the confines of the Roman fort area, which would have provided them with fresh water without leaving the fort.

In the mid-Victorian era many books on Manchester's history were written, and it has to be said, but as kindly as possible, that plenty of them should have been more carefully written. Librarians, historians and vicars

The River Medlock comes out of 'the drop' and continues quietly through the area known as Potato Wharf, down to the River Irwell. The arch on the left is water from the River Medlock and on the right is the overspill from the Castlefield Basin, a unique flower-shaped construction designed to keep the water level in the canal basin constantly at the same height.

The reconstruction of the fort's entrance at Castlefield today. It was kept small so that the fort could not be 'rushed' by large hordes.

were falling over themselves to produce local history books, and some, despite having previously produced good knowledgeable work, grew fanciful and clutched at straws of evidence. Some books were mainly conjecture, including such theories as the idea that the first Roman wooden fort was at the cathedral site on top of ancient Mamecia. The existence of a small Roman 'resting fort' at Sale also later proved to be just one man's imagination. In 1849 someone helping the Ordnance Survey draw a new map of Manchester convinced the map makers that there had been a settlement at Castlefield before the Romans arrived, and so it was shown on that map. Subsequent excavations show that this earlier settlement was just a flight of fancy and its reference was taken off the maps by 1900.

Every time there is a concerted effort to dig into Manchester's past we learn much more about the city's young life. Projects like the Deansgate dig and the Fennel Street excavations over the last 40 years have helped us put the building blocks of early Manchester into place. The trouble is that for every one person who would like time to peer down the construction holes and study what's under Manchester, there are at least two more determined to fill them in with concrete before anyone finds anything that might hold up the construction work.

Traditionally the end of Roman Mamucium came when the Goths invaded the Roman Empire in around 402. The empire started to pull back its legions, and the Romans left the Manchester area completely by around 410. The Brigantes (the locals), who had thought of the Romans as protectors and employers, would have resented their departure.

However, it seems unlikely that all the Romans marched back to Rome and the uncertain welcome that awaited them there. Many of them were fully integrated into their surroundings, and had formed relationships with the locals and had partners and children living with them around the Manchester fort. A sizeable number of men probably did not return to Rome when the orders came. It would have been easy for them to slip into the villages around Manchester and join local communities. Many old Roman customs are woven into the folk lore of the area, and the reason for this probably lies in the men who remained behind.

Chapter Two

MEDIAEVAL
MANCHESTER

IN THE years between the departure of the Romans in the early fifth century and the arrival of the Normans after the conquest in 1066, little is known of the city of Manchester. There is only one written record, the *Anglo-Saxon Chronicle* of 919. It states: 'In the year 923 after the harvest, King Edward went with his forces to Thelwall and... manned it. He commanded another force to take possession of Mamecestre in Northumbria and man it.'

In some areas the communities around the Roman forts grew and became market towns after the Romans left. The Anglo-Saxon period brought the word 'ceastre' to describe where Roman forts had been and all except one, Chester, developed with a prefix denoting the different places – Ribchester, Manchester and Colchester for example. There is evidence that Danes were in the Manchester area in 870. Manchester did not seem to develop into a town, but rather slid back into being an agricultural area of small villages and outlying farms within the *wapentake* of Salford, where the market was the centre of trading. The River Irwell and the Mersey were boundary rivers, with Mercia to the south and Northumbria to the north. The word 'Mersey' means boundary. It is often said that place names reveal the previous occupants of an area, and in Manchester there is evidence of a Danish influence in place names ending in '-hulme', and Anglo-Saxon influence in the large number of names that end in '-ton'.

At one time five areas locally had the name 'hulme', which means 'raised dry land surrounded by boggy ground'. They eventually became differentiated by the addition of prefixes, to become Davyhulme, Cheadle Hulme, Levenshulme and Kirkmanshulme, as well as the original Hulme.

Edward the Elder, son of Alfred the Great, took back the area between the Ribble and the Mersey from the Danes and created a 'hundred'. A statue of him stands in Manchester Town Hall.

There are references to great battles in the area, said to have taken place between 620 and 870. Supposedly the names Nico Ditch and Reddish 'where the river and ditch flows red with blood' and Gorton 'the place of slaughter or gore' come from this period, although the scarce records mean that most such ideas are conjecture and not supported by hard evidence.

King Canute can be traced to the Manchester area just before the Norman Conquest, and he is thought to have given local land to his right-hand man Randalus, an ancestor of the Trafford family long associated with the area. Did they take their name from the area north of Stretford or did they give their name to the area? It has never been proved either way. In 1028 Canute gave licence to 37 towns to mint their own money and Manchester was one of these. Norman village developers chose to continue building Manchester at the confluence of the Irk and Irwell, just as ancient man had long before. They left the Roman part of Manchester untouched. The *vicus* or town outside the fort, which had turned into a farming community, was now known as Aldport – the old town.

When the *Domesday Book* was compiled, Manchester had been paying *danegold*, a poor tax, for some time. It was a poor area relying on the soil for food and animal skins for clothing. The citizens had to pool what little resources they had to survive. A corn mill was eventually built at Millgate in around 930, but Manchester was still not a very big settlement, illustrated by the fact that it did not feature more heavily in the *Domesday Book*. Even the church mentioned in the survey of Manchester is now thought to have been the church in Ashton-under-Lyne.

The Norman Conquest

The Norman Conquest saw the land between the Ribble and the Mersey given to one of William the Conqueror's right-hand men, Roger de Pointevin (Pictou), third son of Roger of Montgomery, cousin of William. He divided the area up into six 'hundreds'. Manchester came under the Salford Hundred and was subject to its laws for 200 years. The area was sub-let to Nigellus, who ruled the whole Salford Hundred. Roger fell in and out of William's favour, eventually supporting a rebellion in 1102, after which he was dispossessed by the king. William Rufus kept some of Lancashire, but let out the barony of Manchester. In 1129 it came into the possession of Albert de Grelly (Gresley) and in 1227 Manchester received a charter for a fair 'On the Eve, Day and Morrow of the Feast of St Matthew'. The fair was held on Acresfield, (now St Anne's Square) and the boroughreeves of the town would guard the entrance to the square and collect tolls on all goods that were brought to the fair for sale. By 1876 the fair had outgrown Acresfield and was moved to Castlefield at the other end of Deansgate.

The Grelleys were an influential family and held lands in Lincoln, Norfolk and Suffolk. They founded a Cistercian abbey at Swinshead, Lincolnshire, and gave it the profits of their mill in Long Millgate, Manchester. They took part in the unrest that resulted from protests against King John and Robert Grelley (5th Baron of Manchester) was one of those who signed Magna Carta. Grelley power finally divorced Manchester from Salford in 1301, and on 14 May that year Grelley issued a charter to 'All my burgesses of Manchester', making Manchester independent. A small agriculture-based village formed the centre of the area, where the people paid service to the lord of the manor with work and animals. The lord fixed the price of bread and ale and none might sell above that price. Manchester got its 'Great Charter' in 1301 and became a free borough. The original area of the barony of Manchester was dictated by rivers, with the Irwell to the west, the Irk to the north and the Mersey to the south, while the Tame marked the eastern limit.

Lancashire had been a royal possession since around 1200, and by around 1351 had its first duke of Lancaster and was a county Palatine, which meant it had the power to raise an army and levy taxes. Robert Grelley, a 'presumptious and fiery baron' decided to move north and live in Manchester, although most of the barons lived in the south and only visited their northern holdings when needed. Robert, however, moved to the area permanently, bringing with him an army of workmen. They built a manor house for him on the site of what was probably Manchester Castle. This was only a wooden fortification and stood where Chetham's College is today. It was Robert who built the first real bridges over the Irk and Irwell and re-built the local church of St Mary. He imported stonemasons, builders, carpenters, gardeners, cooks, grooms and blacksmiths, all of whom were given small plots of land to live on. It was this move that started the growth that led to the formation of modern Manchester.

Robert's son Thomas was a favourite with Henry III and was granted permission (on payment of 20 marks) to chase and kill deer in the royal forest of Salford. On 13 October 1245, the king ordered that five bucks and 15 does from Macclesfield forest be delivered to Thomas Grelley to stock his park at Manchester.

The Grelleys had an unfortunate tendency to die young, leaving youngsters to inherit the family property and wealth. This meant the crown was involved in the administration of the estate. In 1273 Manchester was managed by the House of Lords. In Manchester every burgess (or his eldest son or wife) had to appear, without summons, at the Portmoot, or town meeting, on the four quarter days. In 1301 Thomas Grelley died leaving no heir, and the land passed to his sister's husband Sir John la Warre. Sir John, who with his Manchester bowmen had taken part in the defeat of the French fleet in 1340, as well as playing a decisive part in the Battle of Crécy, died in 1347, aged 69. The West family then inherited the barony of Manchester.

In 1421 Henry V granted a licence for a collegiate church at Manchester and the church in Manchester developed from that grant. Although Salford had been the centre of the old hundred, Manchester had been the religious centre, and there had already been a church in Manchester for over 200 years. The parish of Manchester ran from Ashton in the east to Flixton in the west.

In the early 16th century the lord of the manor was often away on service for the king, and this continued under Henry VIII. It was Manchester's lack of leadership which let power slip to the Portmoot and the church. Manchester had no officials elected by the people, no MP or representative, and was open for visitors and strangers to come and trade and set up in business. Though at the time this was looked upon as a weakness, centuries later it became one of the reasons that Manchester developed as a trading centre and became a leader in the woollen and cotton industry.

There are references to Flemish weavers coming over and founding the textile manufactory in Manchester, and there is a panel devoted to their arrival in the Great Hall at Manchester Town Hall. However, it is not known for certain that this is the case. It seems more likely that Flemish carvers, brought over with money from the Stanley family to build parts of the church, were accompanied by their families, who set up home in England. Warden Stanley set them up in cottages in Long Millgate, and they knew they would be here for many years carving the magnificent woodwork of the choir stalls. The Flemish womenfolk introduced weaving to Manchester, and the art was passed on to the local people. It would have been done firstly to make clothes for themselves, then to make a little extra money. By 1552, 'An Act for the True making of Woollen Cloths' contained a reference to 'Manchester Cottons' and described them as a coarse kind of woollens.

In 1540 the 'Right of Sanctuary' was granted to Manchester, but citizens soon asked for (and were granted) its removal, as there was an influx of criminals and undesirables who came to escape arrest. They stole cloth from the bleaching fields and interrupted trade in Manchester. The Court Leet records were started in around 1550, and some still exist from as far back as 1554. At around the same time the Grammar School, founded by Hugh Oldham, a local man and then Bishop of Exeter, was growing in stature, and education was part of the structure of the community. Manchester at this time, however, was still neither a city, nor a town, nor even a borough. It was still a small market community.

In 1579 John Lacy, a merchant from London, bought the manor from the West family for £3,000 and later, in 1596, sold it to his friend Nicholas Moseley for £3,500. Nicholas's father had been born and grew up in Manchester so he decided to move to the area and build a hall (Hough End Hall) roughly on the site of the house where his father had been born. The Mosleys were lords of the manor of Manchester until the Corporation bought the manorial rights in 1845 for £200,000.

When Nicholas Moseley moved into Chorlton in 1596 he brought stability and a tighter control back to Manchester. He was knighted by Queen Elizabeth in 1599, the same year he was elected Lord Mayor of London. His home here, Hough End Hall, was the family residence for several centuries.

Sir Nicholas began writing his name without the middle 'e' after he was knighted and gradually others did the same. Nicholas Moseley, Lord Mayor of London, became Sir Nicholas Mosley of Manchester.

Hough End Hall as it stands today. The outside is roughly as it was 200 years ago, when it was a farmhouse, and the hall retains much of its original brickwork. The inside has been knocked about by endless disco conversions, cocktail bars, restaurant demands and kitchen additions.

In 1640 Manchester was put forward as a site for a university. The plan was put aside and then forgotten as Civil War gripped the country. Manchester took the side of Parliament against the king, much to the disgust of the Stanleys (Lord Derby) who had land at Castlefield. Alport Lodge was the Manchester residence of the family. It was from that home, which once stood on the southern side of the junction where Deansgate and Quay Street meet, that the Seige of Manchester was launched.

King Street, Manchester. The old Town Hall, by Francis Goodwin (1819–34). It was demolished in 1912, but the façade was re-erected in Heaton Park.

Manchester: looking down on the River Irwell from the Exchange station entrance. The steps were for boat trips. Notice how many shops are on the front of the Palatine Building.

The Museum of Science and Industry in Manchester, which started the successful regeneration of the Castlefield area.

The panel and wall plaques which tell the story of Castlefield under the Romans.

Railway bridge leading from Knott Hill and Deansgate station and spanning the canal, 1978.

The reconstructed Roman wall, with its deep ditch in front as an extra defence.

The entrance to the Rochdale Canal and Duke's 92. The lock-keeper's cottage is above the arched opening.

The canal and railway, both constructed using red sandstone, at Castlefield.

Castlefield is dwarfed by the towering steel and ironwork that carries Metrolink and the railway high over the Bridgewater Canal Basin.

The Middle Warehouse, Castlefield. Built 1831, restored 1992, and seen here in 2000. The two arches were for barges to unload in dry conditions.

The Grocers' Warehouse at Castlefield Basin today. When it was built, over 200 years ago, it used the latest technology and was equipped with water-powered lifts.

The Deansgate Viaduct and
redundant church at the very end of
the Bridgewater Canal, 1999. The
whole of the area nearest the
camera has since disappeared under
new buildings. The church was used
as a recording studio for a time.

Chapter Three

MANCHESTER BEFORE THE CAMERA

Sketches and drawings of the town

Market Place, Manchester, 1833.

Market Street, seen here in 1823 in a drawing by John Ralston.

Mr Hyde's shop, Market Street, roughly 200 years ago.

A busy River Irwell and the wooden 'Actors' Bridge', *c*.1830. The
bridge's real name was Blackfriars Bridge.

Shops on Market Street, Manchester, 1817. Belfast and Sligo
butter is being advertised.

Middle Market Street, Manchester, *c.*1825.

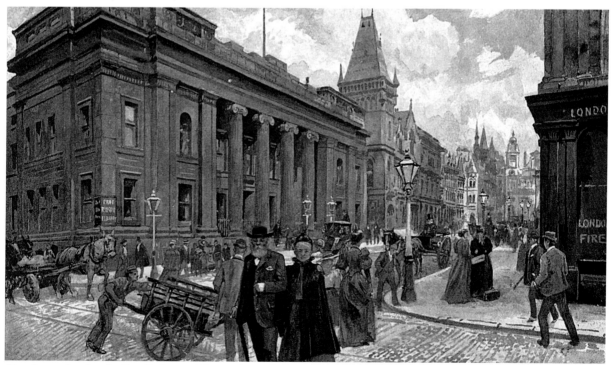

King Street showing the Free Reference Library (formerly the Town Hall) and County Bank in 1890.

The River Irwell between Manchester and Salford, *c*.1800. Coaches would be driven into the water here, then washed.

Old buildings taken down near Strangeways Bridge.

Late Victorian sketch of Market Street, Manchester.

Hulme Hall, which stood where Harry Ramsden's is today.

Ancoats Hall, Ancoats, Manchester, around 200 years ago.

Chetham College and Grammar School from the cathedral yard, 1880.

The cathedral from Hunt's Bank. A busy Victorian scene.

The assize courts, Strangeways, in 1885.

Piccadilly and the Royal Infirmary, a century ago.

Portland Street: warehouses of Messrs Watts and Co. *(left)*, and Messrs Hardy *(right)*.

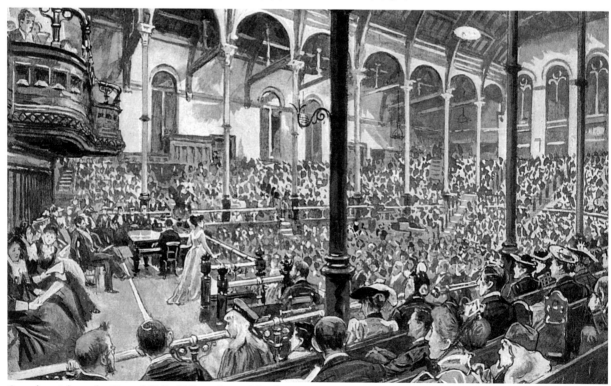

Saturday night at the Central Hall, Oldham Street, Manchester.

The Royal Exchange, Cross Street, in its original form in the 1890s.

The Junction, Hulme: a call to fire. (Upper Jackson Street School is in the background.) The drawing is by H.E. Tidmarsh and dates from 1890.

The Manchester Reform Club, King Street, Manchester. It was built when the Liberal Party controlled Manchester, and is seen here as it was in 1890.

The railway bridge over the River Irwell, Victoria Street, Manchester, *c.*1850.

Chapter Four

THE STREETS OF
MANCHESTER

A look at the main streets of the city over the last 100 years

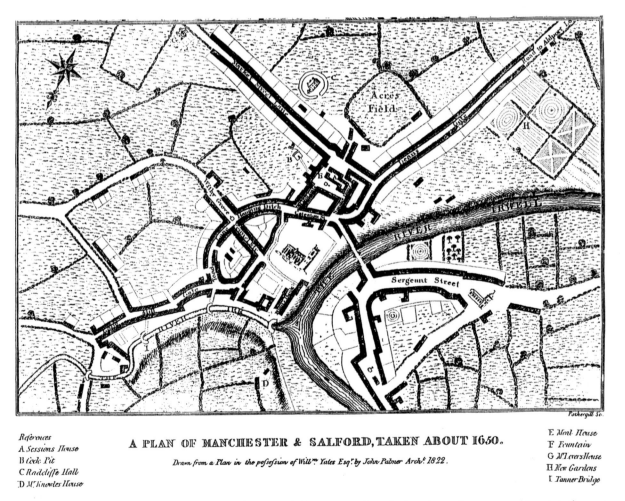

References
A. Sessions House
B Cock Pit
C Radcliffe Hall
D Mr Knowles House

A PLAN OF MANCHESTER & SALFORD, TAKEN ABOUT 1650.

Drawn from a Plan in the possession of Willm Yates Esqr by John Palmer Archt 1822.

E Meal House
F Fountain
G Mr evers House
H New Gardens
I Tanner Bridge

The streets of Manchester and Salford on a map from over 350 years ago. To make it easier to place you need to rotate the page.

A view of the Market Place and the Old Exchange in 1908. The Exchange was the third to have been built on the site and had been visited by Queen Victoria and re-designated the Royal Exchange. The 'original' Exchange was put up in 1725 at the lord of the manor's expense, then pulled down in 1793 because it had become a 'hangout for loungers and ne'r-do-wells.' The street sign affixed to the Wellington Inn says 'Old Shambles'. Samuel Kenyon, the wine merchant, was probably a relation of James Kenyon, whose premises had been on the site since at least 1859. The steps down to the 'Gentleman's Convenience' on the left and the advert for the 'Shooting Range and Skittle Alley' make this an interesting photograph.

Looking from St Mary's Gate into the Shambles area of Manchester, *c*.1890. This view was taken from the first floor of the Royal Exchange, probably on a market day. The stalls look quite permanent and do show up on other photographs of this area taken before 1900. Note though that they are not on the next photograph, taken 20 years later. G.W. Yates Seedsmen is where the back entrance to the new Marks & Spencer store is today. The street alongside runs to the back of Manchester Cathedral. You can just make out the Wellington Inn roof in the middle left of the picture.

Market Place, Manchester, 1912. The stalls have gone and the cathedral can just be made out at the very back of the picture. Yates Seedsmen is still there and the old Shambles building has officially acquired the name The Old Wellington Inn. John Byron, the man who wrote the hymn *Christians Awake* as a poem for his daughter Elizabeth, is said to have been born in this building. Note the pawnbrokers on the left and the extension of the setts in the road.

Piccadilly, Manchester, in around 1890. Note the large open space in front of the Manchester Infirmary, the large domed-building complete with clock on the left. This area, so full of horse buses and horse trams was once known as Lever's Row, after a Mr Lever who lived in a large house later converted into the Royal Hotel. The building is seen here in front of Lewis's. Lever Street in Manchester still keeps his name alive. The royal connection with his hotel came during the visit of Bonnie Prince Charlie in 1745. This area was once the 'daubholes', where clay was dug out to make bricks for the very early Manchester buildings. For some time, from around 1810 to mid-Victorian times, there was a large pond and fountains in front of the infirmary, but these were cleared away to make an area for public statues by 1853.

An early clear, uncluttered view of the Royal Infirmary in Piccadilly. The building had two portico entrances and this reflects the fact that it was two buildings in one. The entrance on the right, below the dome, belongs to the hospital, which had moved here from its original setting in Garden Street (next to the Printworks). The entrance on the left was for the lunatic asylum, which was also part of the complex. There was also a baths and wash house so patients could be cleaned up before being seen by doctors or washed before being sent home. The Duke of Wellington's statue, which was Manchester's second public statue, stands in the foreground. The patients were moved out *en masse* on Tuesday 1 September 1908. A large crowd gathered and watched as around 100 patients walked or were carried to waiting ambulances, carriages, hackney cabs and carts, to move to the new hospital on Oxford Road. One patient was too ill to move, and died the next day.

Piccadilly in 1907. The horse buses have been replaced by electric trams. Many were still open-topped even in 1907 and the picture shows how lightweight the early trams were. They were always coming off the lines and falling over in accidents. The infirmary clock says five to eight, probably in the morning, and the Duke of Wellington stares down on another Manchester day. When this statue by Matthew Noble was unveiled on 30 August 1856, it was called the Wellington Monument. The figures round the base represent Minerva, goddess of the sea, who unfortunately has her hand in the way of Wellington's name, and Mars, sword in hand to represent valour. Victory, with a wreath in her hands, and Peace, with a cornucopia at her feet, are at the back of the monument's large plinth. There are also four relief panels, two depicting Wellington's battles and two depicting his statesmanship and political greatness.

A postcard showing the busy part of Piccadilly, c.1906. The trams are electric but all seen here are the early open-topped ones. On the left we see the spire of Lewis's store and the Wellington Monument. When a competition was held to choose a tribute to the late duke, Manchester's bishop, Prince Lee, was placed in charge of the judging. He made it quite clear that he would not consider any equestrian statues, as the duke's horse was a stallion, and the bishop objected to having an obviously male statue on the streets of Manchester.

Piccadilly in around 1911. Tram No.616 waits to head out to Levenshulme, and its driver is in the open air and exposed to the elements of the city. Ladies did not use the upstairs of these trams as they risked showing a glimpse of leg or stocking as they climbed the open stairs to the upper deck. Later 'modesty sheets' were put on the stairs, attached to the hand rail, as 'young ladies and bright young things' insisted on going upstairs to wave at passers-by on their Sundays out.

Piccadilly *c*.1950. The Piccadilly Hotel and complex is just about to rise next to Parker Street bus station. Three trolley buses wait on the left of the photograph.

An artist's view of how Piccadilly would have looked under council re-development plans first put forward in 1938. The grand colonnaded building was to be an Art Gallery and the open space filled with gardens and fountains. World War Two meant that all the plans were shelved. They were briefly resurrected in 1946, but the shortage of building materials and money ensured they were not realised.

Piccadilly, the heart of Manchester, as it looked in 1936 on a Valentine's postcard. It shows the well laid out gardens and neat lawns. The taller white building, to the left of the centre was at the time the BBC studios for radio in the north. During the war years they moved the studio to beneath the Central Library (now used as the Library Theatre) and many morale-boosting comedy shows were put out from there.

Piccadilly Gardens in spring bloom in the early 1960s. The daffodils and fountains provide a pleasant frame for Rylands (Debenhams') white building on Market Street. The firm had moved into the Rylands building after the fire at their store on Cavendish Street. The buildings left over from the infirmary, which were for a time Manchester's Reference Library, can still be seen in the gardens.

A rare private photo of Piccadilly Gardens in 1937. Lewis's store is behind the Ideal Milk advertisement and the trams are still very much in evidence. Some tram services were actually re-instated during World War Two as they saved on the precious petrol supplies. Here we see a tram waiting to run out to Ashton-under-Lyne, one of the longest journeys on the Manchester Corporation tram system. Little did anyone suspect how much of Manchester would be destroyed by World War Two.

Piccadilly, Manchester at the junction of Mosley Street and Market Street in the 'swinging sixties'. The Wimpy and fast food culture had arrived, in the extension to the Lewis's building. The premises next door, now a large burger outlet, is boarded up and 'to let'. Another new arrival is captured in the photograph and that is the skip. Underneath the 'to let' sign one of Manchester's first skip hire companies delivers what was to be a revolution in house and garden clearance.

Market Street, Manchester in 1906. The horse-drawn trams have long gone, replaced by electric ones, and the independent operators have been replaced by the Corporation. There are still plenty of horses around on delivery carts and cabs. Moss & Sons outfitters is on the left. There was every sort of shop imaginable on Market Street a century ago.

Market Street, Manchester, in around 1890. What a busy and bustling street it was! Horse trams head away from Piccadilly with Longsight, Belle Vue and Hyde on their destination boards. This is the bottom of Market Street and you can see the tram lines of Cross Street running left to right at the bottom of the photograph. Hansom cabs mix with the trams and delivery lorries to present a very busy scene indeed.

Just to prove there is a roadway under those teeming masses, here is a rare photograph of a nearly empty Market Street from a 1905 postcard. It must have been a Sunday morning and some of the shops have their blinds and shutters up to protect goods from the sunshine. Out-of-towners from Oldham, Bury and Bolton used to come into Manchester on a Sunday to window shop in Market Street.

The top of Market Street in around 1926. The original Rylands Warehouse is on the right and Lewis's is on the left. This building in the picture was pulled down in 1929 and rebuilt by 1932 as the white square building with its Wembley-like tower we see in later photographs. By 1926 H. Samuel had moved into the old Rylands building and Finnigans was there as well. Notice the tram lines in the picture. Tram lines have now been re-installed along the same stretch of road, although to cross the road from Debenhams to the ex-Lewis's building today you have to negotiate the recently built Metrolink island platform station.

Above: the top end of Market Street caught on camera in around 1908. H. Samuels is the shop on the right with the clock outside. You can see how the street slopes down toward the River Irwell and the site of Manchester's Market Place. At first the street was called Market Stead (the way to the market), before becoming Marketsted Lane and then Market Street. *Below:* a photograph from the late 1920s taken from one of the offices in the Royal Exchange. The car has arrived on the streets of the city and life will never be the same.

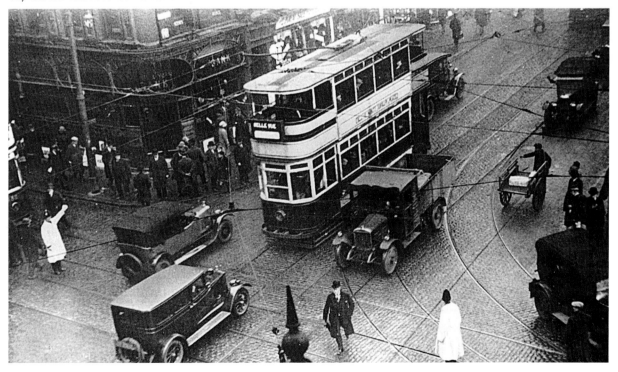

A busy Market Street, *c.*1936, looking up from the middle of the street. The Albion Hotel was one of the famous watering holes on Market Street, as was Yates's Wine Lodge. Yates's started in Oldham but soon moved to other towns and cities in the north-west. The new Rylands building can be seen in the picture. It was completed in 1932 and the architect was P. Gardland Fairhurst, though much of the credit must go to Ted Adams, the project architect, who overcame the problems of a site that was far from square. The new Rylands was designed as a warehouse, with shops on the Market Street and High Street sides. On the Tib Street side, the Piccadilly Restaurant took up most of the street area.

Deansgate, Manchester, in around 1895, at the crossroads with John Dalton Street and Bridge Street. Queen's Chambers is the ornate building in the centre of the view. Built in 1876 as government offices, it has a statue of Queen Victoria on its John Dalton façade. The building is noted for its mullioned windows and Gothic frontage, complete with royal crest over the three-arched entrance. Also visible are horse-trams running down Deansgate. At the time they were controlled by private companies. Corporation electric trams are still some years away. Deansgate means 'the road that runs by the river' and has nothing to do with a church dean or an old gateway.

Deansgate, Manchester, in around 1908, viewed from the city centre end. From the right is the extension to Kendal Milne, then the Victoria Hotel and just peeping out above the gentleman's bowler is Manchester Cathedral. There is still a subway under this part of Deansgate, which ran from Kendal's main shop on the left to what was their linen and household department in the original building, now Waterstone's bookshop. It is a great pity that more was not done to rebuild some of Manchester's great buildings which were damaged during World War Two, such as the Victoria Hotel.

Deansgate, Manchester, in 1929. St Mary's is on the left, St Ann's to the right and Deansgate leads away to the cathedral, which can be just made out in the Manchester gloom. Goodison's was at No.75 and Horan Smith & Co., the fur company, was in Nadin House on the St Ann's Street corner.

Exchange Station, Manchester, and the Cromwell statue, captured on film in around 1886. Manchester Exchange Station is not in Manchester at all, it is in Salford. The River Irwell runs under the bridge leading to the station. The station was opened on Monday 30 June 1884 by the London North Western Railway Company as a solution to the problems of sharing Victoria Station with the Lancashire & Yorkshire Railway Company. On 23 December 1940 the station was completely destroyed by German bombers during the Manchester Blitz. In the photograph a horse-drawn dray and cabs are waiting for their next fare, but it is the statue of Oliver Cromwell that dominates. It was England's first public statue of the man who had led the fight against corrupt royalty. It has been said that this statue was the reason that Queen Victoria declined to come to Manchester and open the Town Hall in 1877. Victoria hated Cromwell, his Parliamentarian movement and all reference to it. The statue was unveiled on Wednesday 1 December 1875 by Mrs Abel Heywood, in memory of her late husband. He was Thomas Goadsby, who as mayor of Manchester had commissioned and paid for the Cromwell statue. He also commissioned and paid for the Prince Albert statue which ended up inside the Albert Memorial in Albert Square. Both were sculpted by Matthew Noble, a leading artist of the time. The Cromwell statue is said to be the best likeness in the world of the Parliamentarian.

Thomas Goadsby was once a worker at the boat yard at this spot. When the launch of a ship called *Emma* went dramatically wrong in 1828, he pulled his boss's two daughters safely out of the river. One of these was Emma, whom the ship was named after, and the other was Elizabeth, whom Goadsby went on to marry. When the cotton famine and the effects of the American Civil War hit Lancashire, it was Thomas Goadsby as mayor of Manchester who fought for the dignity of the people and opposed the means test and oppression favoured by many of his fellow councillors. Thomas was always a 'man of the people' and his actions reflected his working-class background. He never shirked from doing what he thought was right, and was never afraid to put his hands in his pockets to help the more needy. Did he put forward the plan for an Albert Memorial to placate Queen Victoria after the Cromwell upset? We will never know. Thomas died in 1870 and his wife Elizabeth married Abel Heywood soon after. In due course he also became mayor, and she became the only lady to have been the mayoress twice, with with two different husbands.

Manchester has recently altered the plaque on the Albert Memorial and it now mentions Thomas Goadsby for the first time. The Oliver Cromwell statue was moved to Wythenshawe Park in 1968. The sword has been stolen more than once, and is missing at the moment. The statue recently had graffiti sprayed on it. Perhaps it should be moved back to the city centre, to a place more befitting such an historic character.

An unusual view, *c.*1950, of the very end of Deansgate. The street coming in from the right and in front of the cathedral was Victoria Street. The gardens shown here were in the area left after the Victoria Hotel, bombed during the war, had been cleared away. At the time of writing, an office block was rising on this site and the entrance to an underground car park and a collection point for Marks & Spencers were at the far end of this former garden. The Deansgate Hotel seen on the left was the scene of a very mysterious fire during the war years.

Another view of the top end of Deansgate in the late 1950s or early 1960s. The cinema on the left is named the Deansgate (now the Moon under Water pub) with the Deansgate Arcade almost next door. Across the street are Vivian Grant Ltd, the Tudor Galleries and the Barton Arcade, which was put up in 1871. This three-storey glass and iron shopping arcade, produced by a Glasgow foundry, is one of Manchester's little gems.

Deansgate in summer 2000. Now it has cluttered street furniture to guide the lost visitor, 'For Sale' notices, and very obvious road markings.

Oxford Street, Manchester, *c*.1932 – a busy scene with lots of traffic. It must be evening and the queue is waiting to get home rather than into work. The News Theatre on the right was a Tatler and ideal for someone wanting to while away an hour catching up on the latest local news, world news and advertisements. Do not forget that there was no television and this was the nearest one could get to seeing current events.

Oxford Street in the early 1920s. Some photographs are hard to date, and this one features trams built in 1919 and Edwardian-style collars on the gentlemen. The Refuge Tower dominates the back of the photograph. It demonstrates how many imposing buildings there were at the beginning of the 20th century in Manchester. St James's Buildings is the white Baroque-style edifice in the centre of the picture, built in 1912 of Portland stone. It has 1,000 rooms and a very grand marble entrance area, and was built for the Calico Printers' Association. Cotton was king in Manchester, and the wealthy merchants spared no expense in erecting palaces to house their offices and warehouses. Today these huge buildings, now redundant, are being converted into city centre flats and homes.

Looking up Oxford Street from the Portland Street corner, c.1933. The Palace Theatre is on the right with St James's Buildings behind it. The Palace Theatre opened in 1891, designed by one of Manchester's forgotten heroes, Alfred Darbyshire. Alfred loved the stage, and even left the Quaker movement after refusing to give up amateur dramatics. He was asked to design theatres, and it was he, with his famous actor friend Sir Henry Irvine, who came up with the ideas for safety curtains, emergency exit lights, backstage sprinklers and, most important of all, the rule that no place of entertainment must touch any other building on at least three sides. This meant that patrons could get out quickly no matter where they were sitting. He insisted that fire-retardant fabrics should be used, and that steel, not wood, was used in the construction of balconies and upper floors. He was a great hero of the time, but turned down many honours.

He lies, quiet and forgotten, in the churchyard of a church that he had paid for to be rebuilt, Flixton parish church. His headstone has fallen over and is hard to read. But 110 years ago he was cheered on the streets, as his ideas on public safety saved many lives.

The Palace of Varieties was one of the first theatres to incorporate all of his ideas. It was very ornate outside and topped off with large decorated cupolas. These were removed and the look of the theatre was simplified in 1913, then in 1956 it was modernised to the form it still takes today.

'The Cenotaph and Cross', says the caption on this mid-1920s postcard of St Peter's Square. The Cenotaph with its side obelisks is separate from the cross seen in this photograph. The cross was placed there many years earlier, in 1908, to remind people of St Peter's Church, which stood on the site from 1794–1907. The ornate cross was designed by one of England's best Victorian church architects, Temple Moore. Plans were made to build on the land once the church was demolished, but those plans were pushed aside as it was thought that the city centre needed more open spaces. This decision was to prove fortuitous, as it enabled the building of the Cenotaph and Central Library.

A postcard of St Peter's Square just after World War Two. The Cenotaph, which was unveiled to honour those who gave their lives in the 1914–18 war, was due to have a new list of Manchester names added to it. The tram lines and the wires have gone, but the cross and the Cenotaph stand out in front of a very open area. The white building on the left belonged to the Friends Provident & Century Insurance Company, and included Atkinson's and Isaac's Wallpapers.

A photograph of St Peter's Square, Manchester, which must date from 1907. The church of St Peter's has gone, but the cross to commemorate it has yet to be erected. The new Midland Hotel dominates the background. The houses on the right were demolished 20 years later to make way for the building of the Central Library. The open-topped trams confirm the date of this photograph, which was used for an early postcard.

This is an unusual postcard in more ways than one. Firstly, it is a clear and precise close-up of the Midland Hotel, yet it does not seem to be as big or complete as it is today. Secondly, the postcard was actually printed in Berlin, Germany, where many early postcards were printed. However, the card was sent in December 1915, from a wartime hospital ship. Most German-printed cards were destroyed at the beginning of the war, but many seaside shop keepers hid them away until the war was over.

The Midland Hotel had been built on the site of the Gentlemens' Concert Hall. Before that a casino was on this site, and before that it was The Peoples' Hall, which was built in 1853 and pulled down in 1897. The hotel was built by the Midland Railway Company, to balance their great Gothic St Pancras Railway Hotel at the other end of the line in London. Designed by the railway's architect Charles Trubshaw, it was not completed until almost 20 years after the Central Station it was built to serve was opened.

Long Millgate, Manchester, 'the way to the mill', as it appeared in around 1900. The back of Manchester Cathedral is visible at the top of Long Millgate. The mill referred to once stood at the other end of Long Millgate on the banks of the River Irk at a spot now under Victoria Railway Station. The famous Sun Inn can be seen on the very left of the picture, known for many years as 'Poets Corner'. The Manchester Sporting Club was at the top of the street on the left-hand corner for many years.

Outside the cathedral, c.1905. Tram No.457 waits to leave for Belle Vue. Cromwell's statue 'the pedestrians friend', as it became known to traffic dodging Mancunians, guards the middle of the busy road.

The Shambles in the Edwardian era. The café and tea shop is on the left, with china tea priced at 2s 5d and 3s. The old Wellington Inn is occupied by Chambers Electric Suppliers, which took the place of an earlier opticians, and the fishing tackle shop, as the sign 'Worms' confirms. The next building, with its striped awning, was the fish market, and J. Kelsall, Poulterer & Fishmonger, occupied the next building. The cathedral can just be made out in the distance.

St Ann's Square, Manchester, as it looked in around 1914. The Boer War memorial is in place. This statue should be moved to St Peter's Square to be with the Cenotaph.

Hansom cabs dominate this view and this emphasises the fact that this was the shopping area for the richer people of the town. They would patronise the exclusive shops and take their purchases home to the newly emerging leafy suburbs of Manchester. The statue of Richard Cobden was unveiled in 1867, but was later moved to make way for the memorial to the South African wars which was unveiled in 1908.

This postcard of St Ann's Square must be from 1907 because Cobden's statue has moved, but the South African war memorial is yet to appear. The Royal Exchange is the tall building on the middle right. Cobden, as well as his fight for the repeal of the Corn Laws, had done much for the people of Manchester, and had been a major driving force for making Manchester a borough. Because of the narrow confines of the entrance to St Ann's Square it was never part of the tram or bus system and this pleased the cab men of old.

Looking down from St Ann's Church on the square, *c.*1920. This area, which was once known as Acresfield, and was the site of Manchester's Fair, has long been regarded as a centre and meeting place. It was from here that annual Whit Walks started in 1801 and it was here that Manchester's first open-air elections for Members of Parliament were held.

A very early postcard showing King Street from Cross Street, *c.*1903. The old Town Hall is shown clearly on the left. Pulled down to make way for a bank, the façade was preserved and rebuilt in Heaton Park, where it still stands majestically today. King Street was named by followers of James I to show that some people in Manchester were behind him and his efforts to make England Roman Catholic once again.

A 1920s postcard of Oldham Street, Manchester and a glimpse of how busy the street was with shoppers. Although we now think of the street as named after the place it leads to, Oldham, the earlier history books connect the street with the Oldham family, and even Hugh of Oldham, the locally born bishop of Exeter, who left money to local charities.

'Poets Corner, Manchester', says the caption on this postcard from around 1905. The view shows Long Millgate, opposite the Chetham's School entrance, which is where Poets Corner stood. The nickname was applied to the Sun Inn, whose landlord started holding poetry evenings every Wednesday to increase business. The leading Manchester poets of the time gathered there and the readings became a great success. It led to a book of poetry being published, together with a magazine

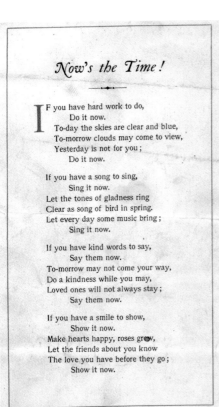

Now's the Time!

IF you have hard work to do,
    Do it now.
To-day the skies are clear and blue,
To-morrow clouds may come to view,
Yesterday is not for you;
    Do it now.

If you have a song to sing,
    Sing it now.
Let the tones of gladness ring
Clear as song of bird in spring.
Let every day some music bring;
    Sing it now.

If you have kind words to say,
    Say them now.
To-morrow may not come your way,
Do a kindness while you may,
Loved ones will not always stay;
    Say them now.

If you have a smile to show,
    Show it now.
Make hearts happy, roses grow,
Let the friends about you know
The love you have before they go;
    Show it now.

One of those poems from 150 years ago, written by Charles Swain from Prestwich, who seems to specialise in advise on how to be nicer in this life. Other Manchester poets who frequented the Sun Inn were John Critchley Prince, J.B. Rogerson, Sam Bamford, and Edwin Waugh.

Albert Square, Manchester, as it appeared between the wars, probably 1936. The traffic is running on both sides of the square. The underground toilets, both Ladies and Gents, provided a much needed and used public service. The Ladies can be seen in the bottom right of the photograph. The buildings on the left of the picture were pulled down in the 1980s and their replacements were built further forward, encroaching on Albert Square. The layout as it is today dates from 1992 and the trees in the square were paid for by the *Manchester Evening News*.

Albert Square, Manchester from an early postcard, in around 1902. The Town Hall is off to the left. The statue of 'Albert the Good' stands in his memorial cover, unveiled on 23 January 1867. The John Bright statue is on Albert's left, put there in October 1891. Nearer the camera is the Victorian fountain, designed by Thomas Worthington and constructed in 1897 to celebrate the successful opening of the pipeline from Thirlmere Reservoir, in the Lake District, to Manchester. This pipeline was a feat of Victorian engineering, bringing clean, pure water to Manchester. The fountain was moved to Heaton Park for many years, but was put back in the square in time for the Waterworks' centenary.

Albert Square from the Mount Street side. A statue of Oliver Heywood is the one nearest the camera in this picture. This joined the Prince Albert Memorial in the square on 11 December 1832. It was sculpted by Albert Bruce-Joy. The Heywood family had done a great deal to improve things in Manchester. Following his father Benjamin's example, Oliver gave a lot of time and money to the city. The open-topped tram dates the picture to around 1902.

Albert Square was created in 1863 purely for the construction of the Albert Memorial. Thomas Goadsby had been mayor in 1861 when Prince Albert died, and he offered the marble statue. Thomas Worthington drew the Italianate canopy for the statue by Matthew Noble, based on the Sir Walter Scott Monument in Edinburgh. At first it was to go in Piccadilly, but that would have meant the infirmary giving up some land, which it was not keen to do.

Manchester had been created a city in 1853 and the Town Hall on King Street was already proving to be too small. Many of the councillors had their eye on an area of council-owned land known as Town Yard, where the Fire Police were, and the town's horses were stabled. They cleared away all the slum property around what was then Bancroft Street and slowly Albert Square emerged. Much of the work on the memorial was done *in situ* by T.R. & E. Williams of Lombard Street, Manchester, and it has provided our city with a wonderful example of Victorian workmanship. The photograph dates from the late 1920s and includes a good view of the Northern Insurance Building, put up in 1902.

Looking up Princess Street from Charles Street Corner in the late 1970s. The railway arch runs over the street which started life as David Street, but was renamed Princes' Street in honour of all Queen Victoria's sons. This was eventually corrupted to Princess Street. The colour printer's on the corner was later transformed into a pub called the Joshua Brooks, a Manchester clergyman immortalised in Mrs Banks's book *The Manchester Man*. Today it is called Sofa and is a lounge bar. The River Medlock runs behind the printers on the left of our picture, and under just where the bus is in the centre of our picture runs the Rochdale canal.

St Peter's Square, 1995. The Central Library dominates this picture, with the Town Hall extension and the Town Hall clock tower peeping over it. This quiet picture belies what a busy junction this is, with the trams crossing in front of the library, heading for Piccadilly, and two-way traffic passing up and down Oxford Road.

Opposite: An early Edwardian view of Albert Square and Manchester Town Hall, opened in 1877 by the mayor Abel Heywood. It had been hoped that Queen Victoria would open the building, but she declined the invitation.

Following pages: Two marvellous aerial views of the streets of central Manchester in the early 1950s.

Chapter Five

THE GREAT BUILDINGS
OF MANCHESTER

MANCHESTER is proud of its buildings and justifiably so. Many were lost in World War Two, notably the Assize Courts at Strangeway and the Victoria Buildings at the bottom of Deansgate. The original Free Trade Hall would have been a fascinating building, and its 1950s replacement will shortly be remodelled.

Every city changes and grows, and people lament the loss of buildings and rejoice at the loss of others. It is good though that so many buildings today are, instead of being demolished, being revamped and used for other purposes. But even this does not suit everyone: for some the thought of a sacred Methodist chapel and meeting place becoming a public eating and drinking venue is difficult to reconcile. However, the huge redundant warehouse buildings that are dotted about the city are now being turned, very successfully, into flats and apartments, so the city centre is coming back to life. Clubs and restaurants are taking over buildings where men and women once slaved daily to earn a living. Hotels are springing up everywhere; the University has grown and spread into the city, café bars line the streets and the whole atmosphere of the city has changed. If anything it is more vibrant, and a new generation of buildings are making their mark. It is very clever the way buildings are stripped to just their façade and completely rebuilt behind, leaving the grand frontage of the Edwardian and Victorian architects. We all want and expect central heating and other luxuries, so the new modern, luxurious buildings of Manchester are rising to the challenge of making Manchester a rival to any city, anywhere in the world.

Manchester's large, grand Gothic Town Hall, seen here on a 1904 postcard. Albert Square and the Town Hall complement each other well. Alfred Waterhouse, the designer, was brilliant in designing the building for the triangular site. The Manchester Town Hall has only three main sides. The fourth is only a few yards wide, thus making it appear a triangular building.

The Town Hall, Manchester, this time looking from Lloyd Street corner in around 1911. The foundation stone of the Town Hall was laid on Monday 26 October 1868, with great ceremony. Copies of some Manchester and Lancashire newspapers were placed in glass in a cavity under the stone, along with coins of the day and copies of the speeches made. Those papers refer to the building as the City Hall, and the invitations to the opening on 13 September 1877 call it the City Hall, Albert Square.

At the time there was a row in the council chambers of Manchester about the name of the new building. 'We are a city now, we need a City Hall' said some. 'We are replacing the old Town Hall with a new one' said Abel Heywood and mayor Robert Neil. Abel Heywood was chairman of the Town Hall building committee and it was his strong will that finally won the day.

Inset: Abel Heywood together with the Great Bell, which hangs with 22 others in the tower. Ten of the bells form a ringing peal and are the same as London's Bow Bells. When the bells first started ringing, the tower had to be re-pointed twice. Each bell has on it the initials of a Manchester councillor of the time, or a council official, together with a line from the poem by Alfred, Lord Tennyson *Ring Out Wild Bells*:

Ring out the false, ring in the true, Ring out the grief that saps the mind, For those that here we see no more; Ring out the feud of rich and poor, Ring in redress to all mankind.

The Great Bell is the fourth largest in Britain and has the initials A.H. and the first line of the poem. There was also a carillon (keyboard) on which tunes could be played on the bells, but it has been broken for some years.

A post-World War Two view of Albert Square and the Town Hall, from around 1950. Can you make out something that looks like a weather vane at the top of the 286ft tower? It is a 3ft gold ball, with spikes, which represents the sun and its rays. The Town Hall took seven years to build and is of brick, faced with local Bradford sandstone. It cost £480,000 including all the fixtures and fittings, which took another two years to put in. There was also the cost of buying additional land and clearing the site, which cost another £300,000.

The Town Hall in 1996 with the banners supporting Manchester's Olympic bid for the year 2000. One thing which impresses visitors to the building is the large great hall, with its famous murals by Ford Maddox Brown. As you walk round the corridors you notice the amount of daylight coming in through the interior windows from the open courtyard in the centre of the building.

Manchester Central Library, St Peter's Square, under construction in 1931. The foundation stone had been laid by Ramsay Macdonald, the Prime Minister, on 6 May 1930 and the building was officially opened by King George V on 17 July 1934. Designed by E. Vincent Harris, the site had cost the council £187,797 and the round building of Portland stone cost £410,000 including fittings (but not the books). It had been open to the public informally since 4 June 1934.

Central Library and St Peter's Square from a 1934 postcard. See how much the cross marking the altar of the old St Peter's church dominates the centre of the square. It was a coup to have King George and Queen Mary open the library and the royal couple worked hard in their few days in the north-west. They opened Birkenhead Library, the Mersey Tunnel and the East Lancs Road in addition to the library. 'To our urban population, open libraries are as essential to health of mind, as open spaces are to health of body,' said King George V in his opening speech. Then the royal couple walked round the corner and laid the foundation stone of the Manchester Town Hall extension.

Because it was designed by the same architect as the Central Library, the squareness of the Town Hall is matched by one side of the extension, yet the curve of the Central Library was matched by the long curved Rates Hall in the Town Hall extension. The 200ft long hall runs down the right of this 1939 photograph taken from the steps of the Friends Meeting House across the road. The railings are still round the Quaker building but were soon removed for the war effort. When the extension opened, both the electricty and gas supplies were in the hands of the Manchester City council, and there were gas and electric showrooms in the building, where you could buy the latest appliances. There was even a small cinema below, where cooking demonstrations and films on health and hygiene were shown. During the war this cinema was used extensively as a training room showing Government films on first aid and air raid precautions.

This photograph from 1937 shows the Town Hall extension nearing completion. In 1934 King George V had pressed the button that lowered the foundation stone into place. It is the block just below the stone ornate filigree work on the buttress nearer the camera. Designed by E. Vincent Hall, the extension was planned as early as 1925, and was intended, along with the library, to be a harmonious development. The circular library (*right*) and the Town Hall (*behind*) make a very impressive picture of civic buildings. A new 62ft conical chamber was built into the extension to reflect how Manchester had grown and taken in the outlying areas of the original city.

The Corn Exchange, Manchester, seen in 1903 from Corporation Street. It is interesting to see the building work going on in front of it, with advertising boards around the site. The Corn Exchange was built in 1837 to a design by Richard Lane, one of Manchester's leading architects. He also designed the Friends Meeting House, Chorlton Town Hall, and Stockport Infirmary. Because the Corn Exchange was built for the commodities business it had to have facilities for horse and carts and later 'lurries' to go down into the basement for loading and unloading. The lifts were powered by water from the River Irwell via the building we now call the Pump House on Bridge Street. The central hall had a glass-domed roof, and food exhibitions were held there and local produce bought and sold. Around the hall were offices, so the whole building was completely compact with everything to hand, as well as being a wonder of Victorian architecture and planning. In more recent times, its vast basement interior has been used for clubs and discos.

Before the building of the Town Hall extension, the offices of the council gas department were in the Corn Exchange, on the Cathedral Street corner. There were also electricity showrooms in St Ann's Square, seen here from a 1929 advertisement.

Here we see the inside of the Corn Exchange in the mid-1980s. At the time it was filled with small colourful shops. Local character Steve stands outside his film exchange shop, looking for his next customer. Joss sticks and incense hang outside Neptune's Cave. The hall was used for postcard fairs, swap meets, fortune telling and record and CD fairs.

Outside the re-vamped Corn Exchange building, artists have created a river bed said to mark the course of Hanging Ditch.

St Ann's Square in 1990. Waterstone's bookshop was formerly Sherratt & Hughes, an old and respected company. Waterstone's was taken over by W.H. Smith when the Arndale Centre closed after the IRA bombing. It was just outside the main door of this shop that Bonnie Prince Charlie reviewed his Manchester Regiment in 1745, and according to old maps there was once a large plague pit just in front of the shop. It was also here that Manchester's first elections for Members of Parliament took place.

Boarded up, shuttered and neglected: the *Manchester Evening News* building on Deansgate. Its official title is Northcliffe House, named after Lord Northcliffe, owner of Allied Newspapers, who built it in 1904. The tower was added and the building enlarged in the late 1920s. It was built as a composing and printing house for the *Daily Mail*, but the *Manchester Evening News*, *The Manchester Guardian* and *The People* were produced here for over 75 years. The buildings are due for demolition in late summer 2001, along with the YHA shop next door, part of the courts, and the Manchester education offices. A new 20-acre complex, including a 300-bed hotel and the new courts of justice, along with the inevitable offices, shops and restaurants, will be built on the spot.

The Shambles area in around 1910, although the postcard describes it as the Old Market Place. The nearest building, now part of the Wellington Inn, was a fishing tackle shop, Chambers & Co. Next to that is the fish market, one of the buildings lost in the Blitz of the 1940s, and William Miller, fish, game and poultry dealers, is on the corner.

The Old Shambles just a few years later than the previous view. The fishing tackle shop has now moved to the first floor, and the Wellington Inn sign now sits above the door. The fishmongers is now a shirt makers and a clock has been installed on the old town house of the Byrom family. John Byrom was born here. He was involved in the 1745 visit of Bonnie Prince Charlie, and his family gave their names to John Street and Byrom Street. Byrom himself wrote the hymn *Christians Awake*.

A view of the Wellington Inn just after the World War Two, probably 1948. The bombed fish market has been cleared away and is now, like so many other bomb sites, a car park. Kenyon's Wine & Spirits is on the corner, with Chambers fishing shop above. The Kardoma Café is behind the Old Shambles clock. The Wellington, named after the Duke of Wellington, in honour of his victories at Waterloo, is just the middle section, next to Sinclair's.

The Shambles as most of us remember it. This is how it was in the 1980s. The whole block was raised 18ft in a re-building programme in 1971. There was, for a time, a makeshift Wellington Inn, which was just a wooden cabin, standing on Cateaton Street. The original building dates from around 1550, though some think it older than that. It is definitely the oldest wooden-framed building in central Manchester. It became a public house in 1830. Sinclair's, next door, was built on the site of John Shaw's Punch House, which opened in 1738 and was famous for serving oysters to gentlemen.

A wet Monday evening in Manchester outside the Wellington in the summer of 1990. This photograph was taken from the back door of Marks & Spencers into what was then called Shambles Square. It was a nice, slightly cut-off area and ideal for meeting friends. All signs of the former clock have gone and the two buildings now cohere into one.

The Wellington Inn and Sinclair's Oyster Bar in their new positions in Exchange Square, Easter 2000. Both pubs were pulled down in 1998 and rebuilt on their new site by Mace Developers, in company with specialists W. Anelay of York, at a cost of £2.5 million. Four joiners stayed with the project for three years, and every bit of the dismantled old timber was photographed and stored on computer, to make sure everything was restored correctly.

This is the old Seven Starrs, and as the sign on the wall says it was probably the oldest licensed house in Great Britain. The spelling 'Starrs' is correct, despite the fact that on postcards it is always spelled 'Stars'. Even in old directories it is spelled 'Starrs'.

Following page:
These two postcards were issued in 1905 and show the charms of the old inn. Reading the type at the side we realise just how antique the place was: Roundheads stayed there, Bonnie Prince Charlie's men were quartered there, and it was said to have a secret tunnel in the cellar. There were plenty of stories and legends connected to the inn. The famous 19th-century novelist Harrison Ainsworth featured the Seven Stars Inn in his book *Guy Fawkes*. Guy Fawkes hides at the inn and makes his getaway through the secret tunnel. Ainsworth was famous for mixing fact and fiction until you could not tell one from the other. Yet for all this history, when the lease ran out in April 1911 the inn was taken down to be sold as ancient building material at auction. A shop was built on the site. It would be interesting to know what happened to the condemned cell door, the leg irons and the contents of the cupboard that had never been opened in living memory.

This room was formerly the meeting place of the Gentlemen constituting the "Watch and Ward." It contains the cupboard which has never been opened within the memory of anyone living. This is shown in the bottom right hand corner of the picture. In here are also to be seen the Old Man Trap, Leg Irons, and the folding doors of the Condemned Cell in the New Bailey Prison, which was sold to the L. & Y. Railway in 1872 and afterwards pulled down. The doors were presented by the Company to the Proprietor of the Seven Stars.

THE VESTRY. "Ye Olde Seven Stars," Manchester
(The oldest Licensed House in Great Britain)

E. T. & Co., Copyright

When in this room one almost expects to hear the arrival of the old Coach announced, and can scarcely conceive such a quaint old room is right in the heart of a huge Modern City. Among many other items of interest it contains a real Cromwell Chair and Table. In 1644 a number of the Roundhead Soldiers were quartered at the Seven Stars, and this room must often have been the scene of their carousals.

THE DINING ROOM. "Ye Olde Seven Stars," Manchester
(The oldest Licensed House in Great Britain)

E. T. & Co., Copyright

Seven Starrs Inn, Manchester.

One postcard of the Seven Starrs that does have the correct spelling. The pub was very popular for meetings, and it is said that beadles, and nightwatchmen would congregate here. 'Time for rounds' they would cry, and drink up, walk twice 'round' the room and then get another round in.

As old as the Seven Starrs was another public house, which claimed that it was older. The Rover's Return was at the top of Shude Hill where the Hen Market stood. The pub claimed that this was 'where they kept the cow that provided the milk for the workmen's brews while they were building the Seven Starrs'.

Central Station, Manchester in around 1905. You can see clearly the covered walkway that continued over Windmill Street and into the back of the Midland Hotel. Central Station was the last of Manchester's main line stations to be built, in 1880. There had been a Central Station at the side of this site on the corner of Watson Street but it was only a temporary affair, opened in July 1878 and closed to passengers three years later. The station was the main terminus for the Cheshire Lines Committee, formed to give Great Central and Great Northern Railways and the Manchester, Sheffield and Lincoln Railways a foothold in Manchester. Trains ran from here to Liverpool and Hull, London and Chester.

The station in 1907. The two black areas at the top were not broken glass but steam vents, to let out the smoke which would gather in the roof from the steam engines.

The Great Manchester Exhibition and Events Centre as it was in 1988 just after it opened. There had been quite a battle in the council chambers over whether to convert the Central Station or build a new exhibition hall out at Belle Vue, on the site of the closed zoo. Eventually they bought the 26-acre central station site in 1978 and plans were drawn up. The area in front of G-Mex, seen here with three steps, seems to have been in a constant state of flux over the last ten years and in 2001, as I write, it is being redesigned once again.

The Midland Hotel, Manchester, built by the Midland Railway Company and designed by their own architect Charles Trubshaw. The hotel was originally meant to be built on to the front of Central Station, but in the end it was built on its own site facing Peter Street, at a cost of £1,250,000. Our view is of the front of the hotel in around 1905, with its profusion of intricate detailing. Begun in 1898, the Midland Hotel was built to equal the St Pancras Hotel in London and is of granite at floor level then terracotta brickwork. The Peterhead pink stone and Shap dark stone contrast well. The site had been the Gentlemans Concert Hall, so the hotel included a theatre. When it opened in September 1903 the hotel had 400 bedrooms, a palm court, a roof garden and its own post office.

A 1919 postcard of the Midland Hotel. The hotel had a covered walkway constructed so that passengers from Central Station who were going to the Midland Hotel did not have to brave any inclement weather. There was also a subway under the road used for the guests' luggage. The hotel closed for restoration in 1985, and is now known as the Crown-Plaza Holiday Inn Midland Hotel, although locals still refer to it simply as the 'Midland'.

John Rylands Library on Deansgate, Manchester, as it stands today. The idea for the building came from John Rylands's third wife Enriqueta. She met the architect Basil Champney at a college library in Oxford and explained that she wanted a building something similar to Oxford, to honour her late husband. John Rylands died in December 1888 and had been one of Manchester's greatest benefactors.

Work began on the building in 1890 and it was always stressed that only the best materials were to be used. It was built of Penrith sandstone and is one of Manchester's finest buildings, and among architect Basil Champney's best. The street on the right of the building is Wood Street, home of the Wood Street Mission which John Rylands supported. When the library was finished Enriqueta Rylands placed her husband's large collection of religious books there, then bought the Althorp Collection from Earl Spencer (Princess Diana's grandfather) for £210,000. Later she also bought a manuscript collection from the Earl of Crawford of Haigh Hall to add to the collection. At first the library was intended to be for the study of theology alone, but after the purchase of the Althorp collection it widened its scope.

The John Rylands Library, just after opening in 1900. The building is well worth visiting and is currently offering tours to the public every Wednesday.

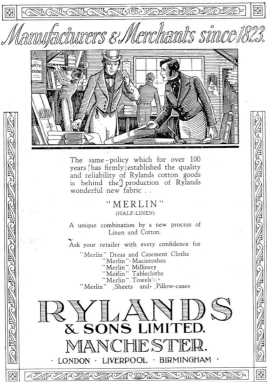

An early postcard of Chetham's College taken in 1904. It shows the boys in their traditional uniforms, in what was the playground. The buildings in the background are very interesting, the low one to the left being the original manor house which Humphrey Chetham left in his will of 1653. The tall tower in the centre is on the original Victoria Railway Station, sadly much modified now. The whitish building with the square windows and small, differently designed towers on top of the square roof is the original Manchester Grammar School, another building lost during the Blitz of the 1940s.

Chetham's College as it would have looked a century ago. Note the uniforms, including hats, of the boys attending the school.

Chetham's Hospital in 1812, from a painting by J. Pawson. The River Irk is coming in on the left.

One of the pupils poses by the well in the inner courtyard of Chetham's in around 1902. Humphrey Chetham, a very wealthy batchelor, was determined that his money was going to do some good for the poor. He settled on education and even during his lifetime had paid for the education and support of 'fourteen poore boyes of the towne of Manchester, six of the towne of Salford and two of the town of Droylsden'. He had been negotiating to buy a college for them when he died in 1653, and left instructions for his executors to carry on his work. He left £7,000 to endow the school, which was a fortune 350 years ago. Children could not have their names put down for Chetham's unless their parents were married, and they had to be (according to Humphrey's will) 'Children of honest, industrious and painful parents and not of wandering or idle beggars or rogues'. The spelling 'Cheetham' was originally used on the front of the card. When the school was officially dedicated on 5 August 1656 the double 'ee' was used on the document, but today, it is always spelled with one 'e'.

Chetham's Library today, one of Manchester's best kept secrets. With over 100,000 volumes, 60,000 published before 1851, it is a national treasure. The largest collection of books and pamphlets on the history of the north-west is housed in this historic building. The library has existed since 1655, is used every day, and welcomes scholars and lay men alike. Marx and Engels sat in this library for hours on end discussing the plight of their fellow man. Harrison Ainsworth sat dreaming of the books he would write – *Lancashire Witches*, *Manchester Rebels* and *Guy Fawkes*. The library has a very special atmosphere.

Manchester's Free Trade Hall, built in 1853 to a design by Edward Walters, one of Manchester's grandest architects. This 1990 photograph shows just the shell of the hall built in 1853. The whole interior of the hall was destroyed during World War Two but was later rebuilt. There was a wooden hall on this site even before the building was opened on 10 October 1856 at a cost of £40,000. The original name for the hall, mentioned on the deeds, was the Manchester Guild Hall, and it could seat 3,165 people. It has been empty and awaiting its fate for the past two years. Every plan that has been put forward seems to involve leaving just the façade and building a large tower block on top. In summer 2001 'sold' notices appeared on the hall.

THIS TABLET WAS UNVEILED BY

HER MAJESTY THE QUEEN

ON THE 16TH NOVEMBER, 1951

WHEN THIS

FREE TRADE HALL

WAS OPENED AFTER BEING REBUILT.

COUNCILLOR WILLIAM COLLINGSON, J.P.,
LORD MAYOR
ALDERMAN A. MOSS, J.P.
CHAIRMAN, TOWN HALL COMMITTEE.
ALDERMAN R.S. HARPER, J.P.
DEPUTY CHAIRMAN, TOWN HALL COMMITTEE

LEONARD C. HOWITT,   PHILIP B. DINGLE,
CITY ARCHITECT   TOWN CLERK.

A close up of the plaque unveiled by Her Majesty the Queen Mother when she opened the re-built Free Trade Hall in 1951. This and the other plaques have supposedly gone into safe-keeping while the hall is sold.

No. 738.   June 26th, 1887.

MR. BIRCH'S
SUNDAY EVENINGS
AT THE
FREE TRADE HALL, MANCHESTER.

Liberty to Obey the Scriptures.

Proving that Romanism does not allow liberty to act
according to the teaching of Christ, and showing the
beauty and simplicity of the Gospel.

PRICE ONE PENNY.

MANCHESTER:
BROOK AND CHRYSTAL, MARKET ST.

The cover of the printed text of a religious meeting held in 1887 at the Free Trade Hall. It was open to all and it was at the Free Trade Hall that the suffragette movement began. Oswald Mosley's 'Blackshirt' movement realised at a disruptive meeting in the hall that the British would not rise to support them. It was also at this hall that Bob Dylan first picked up an electric guitar in public to play the second half of a concert, having played the first half in traditional folk style. The hall has a real place in history and it will be a shame if Manchester loses it.

The front of the Free Trade Hall might have been ornate and decorative with the arms and coats of cities and towns of Lancashire, but the back of the building was very plain, as this 1920 photograph shows. South Street, with its underground gents, is to the right. After the war, when the whole of the inside and most of the back of the hall was destroyed, the Free Trade Hall was one of the first re-building schemes put into action. The back was made more ornate and statues reflecting the arts (including cinema) were put in niches along the back.

Some of the famous people who had played at the Free Trade Hall signed the wall of the changing room under the main stage. Here we can make out Sir John Barbarolli and Yehudi Menuhin, as well as Mick Jagger and The Spinners.

The back of the hall as seen today, including the relief statues incorporated into the back of the hall after the war to break the monotony of the tall brick wall. South Street has now become South Mill Street.

The Royal Exchange from a 1909 postcard, still with its original Corinthian columned entrance. This was the third Manchester exchange to be built. The first two were smaller round buildings. The first one was built in the Market Place in 1729 and the second one at the mouth of St Ann's Square in 1806. This building was opened in 1874 and in 1914 it was decided that rather than move the Royal Exchange they would engage the original architect to enlarge the building. The grand entrance at the Cross Street frontage was taken away, and the side was extended over Old Bank Street. World War One slowed work, and it was 1921 before the building was officially opened by King George V in October 1921.

A lovely view of the Royal Exchange in 1907 seen from Cross Street. Manchester's first telephone exchange was above the offices here, useful as so many of the calls would have been to and from the cotton dealers. There were 500 brokers, 1,800 yarn agents and 1,800 cloth merchants registered here at the time of our view. They met every Tuesday and Friday and had a system of reference letters and squares marked out on the pillars of the hall so they could locate each other.

An ornate building on the corner of Red Bank and Miller Street, which was built in around 1904 as headquarters of the Co-operative Insurance Company. When the Co-op moved out into their new skyscraper, it became Parker's Hotel and later Parker's apartments, one of the first 'Live in the city centre' rejuvenation schemes.

Piccadilly and the top of Market Street, Manchester, *c*.1912. The tower of Lewis's Department Store shows up very well on this picture. Lewis's was built between 1878 and 1880 on the site of the Royal Hotel. This was Manchester's first large retail store, and has been building, re-building and spreading ever since it opened. David Lewis opened his first store in Liverpool, and was very aggressive with his advertising. This was the first time people could actually walk round and touch the goods rather than being handed them by an assistant. Although Lewis's has now gone, it really has a place in Manchester's history, and the tales and stories of the displays it put on are legendary. It had the largest soda fountain outside America, the first escalators outside London, the first radiators with thermostats and a dance floor completely mounted on springs. Christmas didn't start until Father Christmas arrived at Lewis's and the grotto there always outshone all others. One year they flooded the basement and Santa's helpers pulled the little visitors across on a raft to visit 'Christmas Island'. Later the same idea was used to recreate Venice in the basement.

Lewis's, Market Street, Manchester. Where the arcade sign is on the left was once a separate street.

The interior of Lewis's Modern Restaurant, captured in 1912. Among the things that have been on display in Lewis's window are a Zeppelin carriage, a Spitfire plane, and Donald Campbell's *Bluebird*.

Market Street, Manchester, with Lewis's and Rylands' Stores defiantly facing each other. Lewis's was definitely the leader – it was the first and the most innovative. Davis Lewis, who started the firm, was born in 1823. He had no children so brought in nephews (Cohens) to help run the firm. He believed in advertising in a big way, and was the first to take out display advertisements in local newspapers. He believed in putting the price on the goods and not bargaining, as other stores and shops before him had. He would print his own-brand exercise books, cash books and even novels at a cheap price. When David Lewis bought land in Manchester in 1878 he had in mind a plan to build and build. By the time the store opened in 1880 there were 300 people working in the suit-making department and about 250 in the shoe-making department. When Lewis's first opened it was a department store for men and boys, selling suits, shoes

and accessories. Ladies' fashions came along later. When David Lewis died in 1885 the store had already been rebuilt and enlarged. In 1912 the foundation stone of a new building at the back of Lewis's was laid, and in return for giving up seven foot of frontage on Market Street, the council allowed them to enclose Meal Street, which ran between them and Piccadilly. The building we see today is a 1929 rebuild that enclosed another of Manchester's old narrow streets.

Manchester's 26-floor Co-operative Insurance building, the tallest building in Manchester and, when it was erected, the tallest in Europe. This view is from Cateaton Street and shows the dome of the Triangle (Exchange) in the foreground. The CIS is 400ft high and said to weigh 100,000 tonnes. It has 13 acres of floor space and 250,000sq ft of window, the glass weighing 300 tons. Fourteen million pieces of Italian mosaic were placed by hand in the self-cleaning entrance. The foundation stone was laid on 13 July 1960 and the building was officially opened by the Duke of Edinburgh on 22 October 1962. It sways two inches each way in a high wind.

The fire station on London Road and Whitworth Street, Manchester, seen here on a postcard from 1910. It is a triangular building, built of red brick and yellow terracotta. Begun in 1906 it is large and impressive, designed by Woodhouse, Willoughby & Langham. When the building opened it was new in concept because the firemen and policemen lived in the station, complete with their families, so that they were always ready to answer a call. It was found to be too big and old fashioned in the 1960s and at the moment it seems likely that it will be converted into a hotel.

The Albert Hall and Aston Institute on Peter Street, Manchester, opposite the Free Trade Hall and built by the Manchester & Salford Wesleyan Mission. They had been holding meetings known as 'Pleasant Sunday Afternoon' (PSA) and filling the Free Trade Hall every Sunday. So they decided to build their own meeting place, and in 1910 built the Albert Hall. It had a large hall on the first floor with stage, pulpit and row upon row of seating for 2,000. The upkeep of the hall was proving expensive, and the congregation had moved away from the city centre. Though organised coaches and trips to the Albert were popular on a foggy night, the hall was almost empty. On Sunday 6 June 1971 the congregation met for the last time and, joined by the congregation from Central Hall in Oldham Street, they walked from the Albert to Central Hall, closing the doors behind them. One little note from history is that as news of the Munich air disaster spread through Manchester, people started to head for the city centre to be kept up to date with the latest news. It was at the Albert Hall that they gathered and hundreds gathered in the hall, while thousands stood outside and runners kept the ordinary people of Manchester informed. It was here that the large memorial service was held for those who had died that day. Today the building is a bar, Brannigan's, 'for eating, drinking and cavorting'.

The same view today and although the building has been saved by First Leisure, who have taken a 25-year lease on the Albert Hall, the meeting hall, which can hold 2,000 people on the first floor, seems a wasted space. The rostrum, stage and seating is all still there, but electric light fittings for downstairs protrude through the floor and the area cannot be used. So much of Peter Street has become home to bars and clubs that it must soon reach saturation point.

Manchester's Technical Institute, Whitworth Street, as seen in 1912. It later became known as the Sheena Simon Institute and is now part of the City College.

The Royal Infirmary, Manchester from a 1912 postcard. An ornate and very distinctive building, it was built in 1905 to replace the crowded buildings in Piccadilly. The movement of patients was done with much publicity and only one patient was deemed too ill to move.

The Royal Infirmary, Manchester, from a 1925 postcard. The royal patronage was granted by William IV in 1830. The hospital was built on the pavilion plan over 13 acres of land after the university, which owned the site, invited the hospital to move here. Because the Eye Hospital and St Mary's Maternity Hospital also moved here, most of central Manchester's hospitals were on one site.

The School of Art, Cavendish Street, All Saints, Manchester, built in 1881 to a design by George Tunstall Redmayne. The list of pupils and teachers here is very impressive, with Winstanley, Randolfe Caldicotte, Walter Crane and Richard Sickert among them. The building, seen here in 1890, is now part of the university.

The Courts, Aytoun Street, Manchester, built between 1869 and 1873 as the police and sessions court. Designed by Thomas Worthington, they incorporated many new features. A strike by the builders for over a year delayed the opening and the costs spiralled to £81,000 from an estimate of £37,000. It had special sealed corridors so witnesses could come and go without being seen from the public gallery. It had cells, each complete with WC, and these led up to the dock in the centre of court. The four courts were in the very centre of the building, making escape harder. The officials had a separate entrance so as not to mix with criminals and the public. In times past Fenian prisoners were even smuggled out on to a barge on the Rochdale Canal that runs alongside the building. I toured the building from top to bottom just before work began to modernise the building in 1996, and it was an eerie sensation. There were small cells, heavy doors, heavy bars and spikes on top of many surfaces. It is now referred to as a Crown Court and will be taking on a lot of cases as the Crown Square courts are rebuilt.

The Medical School, Manchester University/Owens College. The Manchester Royal School of Medicine was incorporated into Owens College in 1872, and work started on the Medical Hall, incorporating the Library of the Manchester Medical Society of 80,000 volumes. On the left were the Roscoe Laboratories and Schorlemmer and Morley Labs.

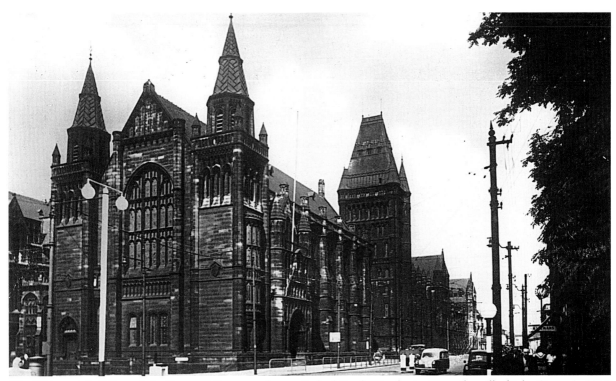

The Whitworth buildings of the Owens College complex on Oxford Road, Manchester. From the will of John Owens in 1857 a college, for all religious denominations, was started at his house in Quay Street, Manchester. It was enlarged in 1870 and moved to Oxford Road in 1873, becoming the Victoria University in 1880. A Liverpool branch was added in 1884, and Leeds in 1887, but as they grew they broke away and became independent, leaving Manchester as a university city in 1903. Alfred Waterhouse was chosen as the architect in 1869 and work began in 1870. It was 10 years before the Quadrangle was complete and it was Alfred's son Paul who completed the 1912 museum addition and the 1927 extension.

Manchester Assize Courts, Strangeways, seen here on a postcard from 1906. This was Alfred Waterhouse's first commission in Manchester, and opened for the Assizes for the Hundred of Salford on 25 July 1864. Lord Chief Justice Cockburn took the case, which included sheep stealing, bigamy, concealment of a birth, arson and stealing a postbag and letters. It was the success of this building that

led to more work in the city. He designed more of Manchester's great Victorian buildings than any other architect. It was said at the time that no matter what class of Mancunian you were, you would enter a Waterhouse doorway during your lifetime. He designed the Town Hall, the Refuge Insurance, the university, the convicts entrance at Strangeways jail, and churches. This view seems to be the opening of the Assizes as there is a coach and finery and a waiting crowd. There were statues in the niches and these were rescued after the building was hit during the Blitz of 1940. Unfortunately Manchester decided not to re-build the court and it was cleared away in the mid-1950s.

Alfred Waterhouse did more than build grand civic buildings. Here is one of his lesser known works, the cold storage building and abattoir on Water Street, near to where Harry Ramsden's is today.

The Great Northern Railway Goods Warehouse, pictured here in 1995 just before conversion work started.

Chapter Six

CHURCHES AND THE CATHEDRAL

T HE DATE that Christianity arrived in the Manchester area is uncertain. The mural in the great hall of Manchester Town Hall shows the baptism of King Edwin of Northumberland, in the early 600s, taking place in the area. Some history books place Edwin in North Wales, away from the Danes, when his conversion took place. Certainly by 669, when St Chad had become bishop of Mercia, there would have been some form of church in Manchester, even if it was only a wooden 'house of prayer'. It is probable that such a building was in St Ann's Street near Cross Street. However, in the period between the Romans leaving and the Normans arriving, very little was written down or passed on verbally, and 300 years of history is largely unknown to us now.

The River Mersey was the boundary between Northumberland (all the land to the north) and Mercia (the heathen area to the south). It seems likely that Christianity waxed and waned on both sides of the river, depending on the views of successive lords of the manor. Lancashire and Cheshire had not been created at the time.

It is very likely that the first church was dedicated to Our Lady, St Mary the Virgin, mother of Jesus. The second church, built in Saxon times, would have had the same dedication and probably stood where Barton Square runs into St Ann's Square. The shop Sports Pages is roughly on that spot today, in the Gardens Building. This second church is remembered by the name St Mary's Gate.

A view of the cathedral from the corner of the Corn Exchange in 1929. Notice that this southern side was far more elaborate than it is today. The Chantries, St Nicholas's founded in 1350 and St George's founded in 1501, were not rebuilt after being

damaged during World War Two. In 1845 King William IV appointed commissioners to look into areas that they thought would be suitable to be made bishoprics. Manchester and Ripon were put forward in a report that came out on 4 March 1836, but was suppressed by the Government, which was worried about bishops voting in the House of Lords. It was not until 10 years later, on 19 April 1847, that Manchester finally became a diocese. *Right*: The cathedral and the area around it, as it looked in 1904.

A view of Manchester Cathedral and Fennel Street, as seen on a 1907 postcard. Note the Cathedral Hotel on the left hand side of Fennel Street, and what was Manchester Sporting Club behind it. Looking up Fennel Street, Thomson House (the Printworks) has still to be built. The porch on the front of the church was added in 1896 to celebrate Queen Victoria's Jubilee, and was known at the time as the Victoria Porch, completed in 1897. The tower as we see it is a rebuild from 1864.

The cathedral and Chetham's School behind. Manchester Grammar School stands out clearly behind the tower. Our photograph is from around 1901 and the Victoria Porch, along with the choir rooms either side, is still showing a clean light face.

The Reverend Joshua Brookes. Not one of the bishops of Manchester, but certainly one of the more colourful characters associated with the old church. Born in 1754, his name is entered in the register as being baptised on 19 May that year, but the problem is that the entry is in his own handwriting and at the bottom of the page out of date order. One can almost suspect him adding himself just for the sake of vanity. He was actually baptised at Cheadle. Jotty, as he liked to be called, was a character in every way. When baptising babies, if he did not approve of the name the parents were bestowing on the child, he would just go ahead and change it during the ceremony. One such famous case was recorded in the book *Manchester Man* by Mrs L. Banks. She tells of an orphaned child, who was pulled out of the River Irk, and was about to be christened with the name Irk, but Jotty had other ideas, and called the baby Jabez, a name taken from the Bible. The stories of Joshua Brooks are legendary, and include stopping a funeral while he went for more toffees (horehound drops) and boxing the ears of a bridegroom for kissing the bridesmaid too enthusiastically.

A view of the interior of St Benedict's Church, Ardwick, *c.*1910, showing the high altar and east window. The church was paid for by Councillor Bennett, whose name was given to the street outside. It is a very 'high' church, and was once attacked by Protestants who thought it was Roman Catholic.

St Ann's Church in St Ann's Square is a popular and busy church right in the city centre. In around 1706 Lady Ann Bland (née Mosley) decided that she was not happy with the vicar at the parish church (the cathedral), whose name was Richard Wroe. She applied to Parliament to build her own church in 1708, and on 17 July 1712 St Ann's Church was consecrated by the bishop of Chester. We now think that John Barker was the architect, but local folk history says Christopher Wren had a hand in its design.

Above we see the church as it is today, and *below left* is Christmas 1932, and the church is decorated with a christmas tree and presents for poor children. A bomb landed right on the church tower during the war, but did not explode, so the church was saved. *Below right* we see a photograph of the Lady Chapel taken in the 1920s.

St Mary's Roman Catholic Church in Mulberry Street, Manchester, known to all as the 'hidden gem'. Built in 1848 and now a Grade II listed building, it was designed by John Gray Weightman and Matthew Hadfield. There was a church or meeting place for Roman Catholics on this spot before permission was given for the building of the new church. The design has been much criticised by other architects, and yet over 150 years after it was built, it has a firm place in the hearts of many Mancunians. *Below:* part of the wonderful alabaster and marble interior. *(Photograph V. Gillibrand)*

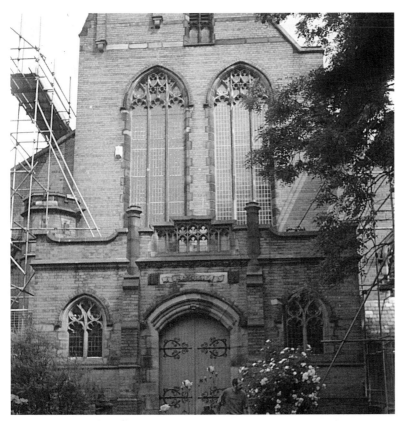

Christ Church, Moss Side, undergoing repairs in 1999. This church has had a chequered history. As an Episcopal Chapel it was put up for auction with a reserve price of £3,600, but no one showed any interest. One of the curates of this church was George Garrett, who invented the world's first submarine. Much of the money raised to build the submarine in Birkenhead came from garden parties held at the church.

St George's Church, Hulme, photographed on the day that the Mancunian Way flyover was demolished in 1998. Started in 1826 to a design by Francis Goodwin, it was one of the churches paid for by Church Commissioners to celebrate the victory at Waterloo. It was a cavalry church, and served the barracks which stood nearby on the other side of Chester Road. Many of the graves in the churchyard are those of officers killed in action. After standing empty for many years, the church is now being turned into modern apartments.

St Francis's Roman Catholic Church, Gorton Lane, Gorton. This church was also the monastery for Franciscan monks who moved to Manchester in 1861. The photograph shows the monastery and surrounding streets as they were in 1948. The towering Gothic church is one of E.W. Pugin's designs, and is now a listed building.

After standing empty for many years, and after failed attempts to turn it into flats, the church is now in the hands of the Monastery Trust who plan to restore and find an alternative use for the building, which is Grade II* listed. The project has been called 'The Angels' and is a community-based project for the good of those who live in the surrounding area.

Gorton Monastery, the church of St Francis, showing how it dominates Gorton Lane, and the surrounding area. The buildings nearest the camera are what remains of the monks' quarters. Plans for this church include a Red Cross training centre, a crèche and playgroups and doctors' surgeries, all intended to help with the regeneration of the area.

A close-up of the Crucifixion, high on the tower of St Francis's Church, Gorton.

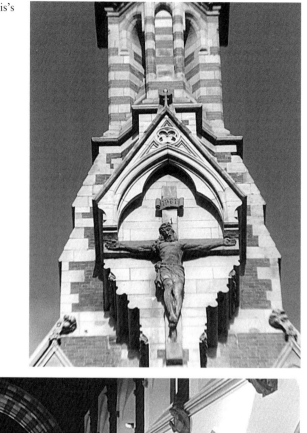

The interior of Barton Monastery, 2000. It was designed and built by E.W. Pugin, just a few years after the completion of Gorton. Many features here are repeated from Gorton's St Francis's.

Chapter Seven

TRANSPORTATION: TRAMS, TRAINS AND BUSES

THE RIVERS Irwell, Irk, Medlock and Croal were ancient man's highways in the Manchester area. The Romans forged their own pathways across the land. Later still, men rode on horseback, and struggled with carts down the muddy drovers' tracks. Then in about 1755, one Francis Egerton arrived in the area, having been shamed at court by the fact that his fiancée's sister had been going out with a married man. He settled here in the north west, where he had inherited some land at Worsley. John Gilbert was his estate manager, who also looked after the business of coal mining on the estate. It was probably John Gilbert who came up with the idea to drain the mines and use the water to transport shallow coal barges, but it was James Brindley, the whizz-kid of the time, who made the plan a reality.

By around 1770 a canal had been cut from Worsley to Castlefield, in Manchester. This new mode of transporting coal brought the price of it down, and a new era in transport had begun.

Canals were ideal for all kinds of transport. The agricultural plains of Cheshire were a prime site for the development of the canal system. All manner of produce could be easily transported along this new man-made highway. Vegetables from the farms of Cheshire were ideal cargo for the new system. So the Duke of Bridgewater extended his canal through North Cheshire, and eventually on to connect with the River Mersey, in Liverpool, and from there the whole world.

Castlefield Basin entrance in 1990. Note how the railway arches have been put to many uses. The canal narrow boats, once used for transporting coal and potatoes, are back, but are now mostly used as pleasure craft. Garden sheds and old caravans still appear as offices and sleeping accommodation: every bit of land is valuable so near to the city centre.

A busy picture showing the Castlefield Basin of the Bridgewater Canal during a boat rally in 2000. Canals, in general, are coming back to life, used mainly for pleasure, but also making a peaceful backdrop to the newly emerging regenerated area of Manchester. This photograph shows the grand railway bridges, complete with 2-car DMU, which were constructed to get the railway across water.

A quiet moment at Castlefield at Easter 2000. Merchant's Bridge, built in 1996, spans the Bridgewater Canal. All the new development has brought life back into the city centre. People can now live here, and walk to work. The canal system, put in place 200 years ago, has proved to be a boon to modern Manchester.

Piccadilly, Manchester, in the late 1890s. This picture was taken before trams became electrified, when horsepower ruled. The first horse-drawn omnibuses in the area were in Pendleton, Salford to Failsworth Pole. Picture postcards first appeared in the early 1900s, but some, like this one, featured in much earlier photographs.

Deansgate, Manchester, in 1904, demonstrating how one slow tram could hold up a whole line. When there was a breakdown, which thankfully was not often, horses and passers-by had to be persuaded to push the tram into a cross-over point or siding.

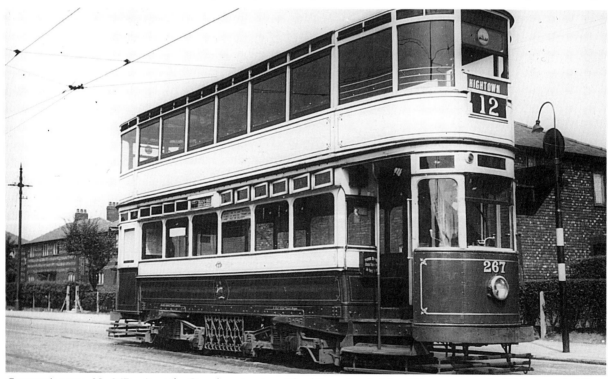

Corporation tram No.267 waits at the Greenheys terminus, Lloyd Street South, Moss Side to start out for Hightown, via Albert Square, the No.12 route in April 1938. Hightown was off Waterloo Road, Cheetham Hill and was a popular destination as it was a very built-up area. *(Photograph H.B. Priestley).*

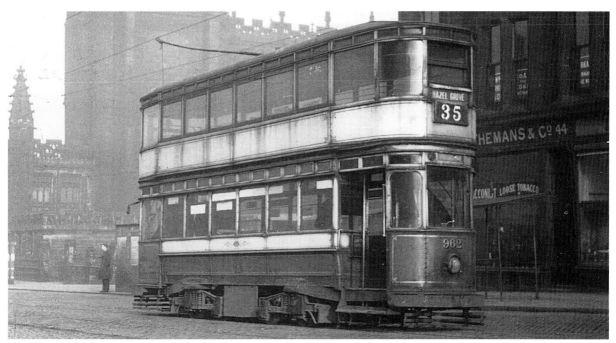

Trams advertised as leaving Exchange Station had their terminus at the cathedral. It was quite a busy spot and a number of routes and services started here. Here we see tram No.962 waiting to leave on that long journey to Hazel Grove (route No.35) in the foggy mist of 9 January 1949, the last day before buses took over. *(Photograph John Fozard)*

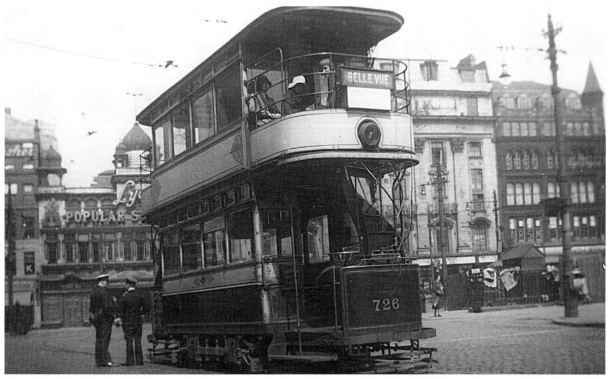

Piccadilly, Manchester, 1932: a Sunday morning and the Corporation tram number 726 waits to head out to Belle Vue and all the promised pleasures there. Sunday was the day that brought out the old stock while repairs and services were undertaken on the more modern fleet. The tram here is an 'open-balcony' type and would have been in service for over 20 years.

Albert Square, Manchester was a busy tram terminus and here we see the scene from the 1920s. Open-balcony trams wait to leave for Hightown (north) and Chorlton-cum-Hardy (south) and though the pavements are wet there are no tram shelters for the waiting travellers. Note the 'Parcel Receiving Office' sign on the left. Parcels could be sent by tram, as long as you bought a ticket for them. You could send parcels all over the Manchester area via the tram system.

Rush hour, 1946. Trams wait on Oxford Road to head into the city centre and take workers home.

An early Manchester tram from around 1912. You can see the balconies have just been filled in and it is now completely enclosed.

One form of transport from the past that seems to be largely forgotten is the trolley bus. The trolley bus was powered by overhead electricity lines so it was cheap and clean to run and did not require the expense of laying tram lines and digging up the street. Most of Manchester's trolley buses ran east and north-east to Hyde, Denton and Ashton-under-Lyne. Here we see an Ashton trolley bus turning from Portland Street, Piccadilly into Aytoun Street in around 1959. The advertisement on the trolley bus is for Cheetham's Transport (the Snipe, Audenshaw) service to Bristol and South Wales. Trolley buses were introduced into the greater Manchester area in Stockport as early as 1913 but they were not popular. The solid tyres and unreliability caused problems and they were stopped in September 1920, in Stockport.

Trolley bus No.1251 in Portland Street c.1960, waiting to leave on the 210X service to Denton via Ardwick and Belle Vue. The 'X' denoted that the bus was not going to complete the whole of the 210 route to Ashton-under-Lyne. The 'X' was used for rush hour traffic and would free the regular buses and trams for people wanting to take the whole route. Manchester's first trolley bus service began on 1 March 1938 on the Ashton Old Road route. Twice the Transport Committee voted to replace trams with buses and twice the council over-ruled the decision, opting for trolley buses. Their argument was that the electricity was generated by the Corporation and the infrastructure was already in place. As it turned out, this was the right decision, as during the war petrol was in short supply. The trolley buses ran right through the war.

In Manchester the mixture of trams and buses was a fascinating one. As both modes of transport were controlled by the Corporation, they decided when to phase out trams in favour of buses. However, during World War Two many tram routes were re-introduced, and tram lines were even re-laid on Princess Road because of petrol shortages. Electricity for the trams could be produced from local coal. Here we see the interior of the Hyde Road depot in around 1931, and there is a mixture of trams and buses in the repair shop.

A Manchester Corporation bus, the latest to join the fleet, in 1929. The driver was shut off in his cab and it was left to the conductor on the platform to sort out the passengers and collect the fares. His was a job only for the fit and healthy, especially during rush hour.

Corporation Street, Manchester, in the 1950s. Buses pass the Corn Exchange *(left)*, Thomson House and the Co-op *(centre)* in this busy scene.

Belle Vue, Manchester, in around 1930. The scene is Hyde Road, near the Lake entrance to Belle Vue Gardens. Mona Street, later Edward Street, is on the left. The street is busy – it is a typical working day.

Lower Mosley Street Bus Station was where most Mancunians left from when taking longer journeys. Trips to Blackpool, Yorkshire, Scotland and London all began here, at the basic bus station with a transport café. The site is occupied by the Bridgewater Hall today. Here a North Western Road Car Company bus is waiting to head out for Yorkshire (Leeds and York), in around 1950.

A Corporation bus on Mosley Street, Manchester on the No.23 route to Piccadilly, c.1947. Note that Manchester buses carried advertisements on the side, something that Salford buses never did.

A Manchester Corporation bus waits in Piccadilly, ready to run a short service down to Old Trafford. These short services and specials always carried a letter, and the football specials were usually 11X, as seen here in a 1950 picture.

A rare photograph of Liverpool Road railway station just after it was closed by British Rail on 8 September 1975. Today it is the Museum of Science & Industry.

The interior of Victoria Railway Station 100 years ago. It is 9.20am, so salesmen and representatives are heading out to complete a day's business. Only the bosses and shoppers are still to arrive.

The view of the approach to Manchester's Victoria Railway Station in autumn 1960. The building on the right was a flower shop with a night club above. Started by the Manchester & Leeds Railway in 1844 as Hunts Bank Station, the Lancashire & Yorkshire Railway Company enlarged it and built Victoria Station, once the largest station in the country, in 1845.

Manchester's rail system suffers from the fact that the north and south of the city were developed by different railway companies and plans were never put forward for them to work together and be integrated. The Passenger Transport Authority for Greater Manchester was set up in 1968 and its job was to bring all forms of transport together. They put forward proposals for an underground for Manchester, rather like Liverpool's system, where the ordinary lines coming into the city dip and continue across the city at a low level (underground). A lot of money was spent on planning and even on the compulsory purchase of property. At the last minute the Conservative government withdrew all funding and the scheme collapsed.

The platforms of the Liverpool–Manchester railway station at Liverpool Road, Manchester as they were in 1900. Passenger trains had long since moved on to Victoria Station, and the yard was used as a goods depot, gathering parcel traffic from the Manchester area. The site was sold to the GMC in 1978 for £1 and work started in June 1979.

Liverpool Road Station today. It is now part of the Museum of Science & Industry, and while most of the building is offices and workshops, the original station entrance has been restored as it was on its opening day in 1830. The first part of the museum opened in 1984, five years after work began clearing the site.

The award-winning Museum of Science & Industry, Manchester, is one of the largest transport museums in Great Britain. The main exhibition hall, the Power Hall, was once the goods shed for the Liverpool–Manchester railway when it opened in 1830. After the passenger traffic moved out after less than 20 years, Liverpool Road Station became the Parcel and Small Goods Receiving Depot for Manchester, and continued in that role for over 100 years, before being sold for use as a museum for a peppercorn amount.

The approach to London Road Station as it was in around 1908. This station opened as a permanent station on Tuesday 10 May 1842. The first train was to Sandbach, the end of the line, and it was 10 minutes late departing. There had been a temporary halt two miles down the line while this station was being built by the Manchester & Birmingham Railway Company. Quite a few small railway companies were allowed running rights into the station, including the Manchester, Sheffield & Lincoln Railway, but most had been swallowed up by the giant London & North Western Railway by the time this photograph was taken. The original station was rebuilt in 1860 and again in 1880, and it is this later building which is seen here.

Central Station, Manchester, on a 1930s postcard. The covered walkway linking the station with the Midland Hotel is clearly visible. As the signs suggest the Cheshire Lines Railway Committee and the London North Eastern and London North Western shared the station.

A charming study of Central Station seen through the locked gates just after it closed in May 1969. For some years it was used as a car park until plans for it to be transformed into the exhibition centre G-Mex were put forward.

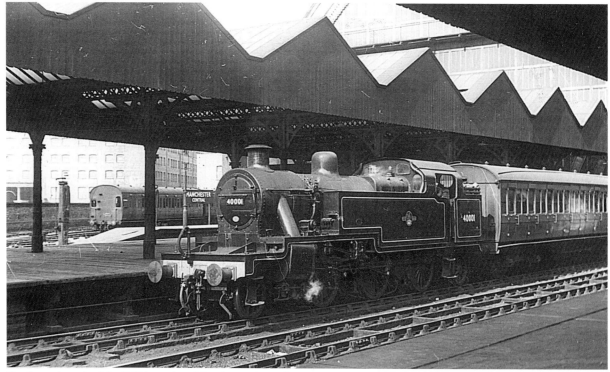

Fowler tank engine No.40001 stands at Manchester Central in 1957 waiting to depart for Liverpool Central, all stops. The very distinctive pointed awning of the platforms outside the station is shown clearly on this photograph.

Manchester Central, 1965. A short train waits to depart through Chorlton for Tiviot Dale Stockport. All three engines seen on this picture were Fowler tank engines, built in 1927. There were almost 650 engines in this class and they were the workhorses of the short and stopping trains out of Manchester Central.

A London North Eastern Region Express comes into Manchester Central Station in the 1930s.

The inside of Central Station, just six months before it closed. By 1968, when this photograph was taken, many of the services had been moved away to other Manchester terminals. Here we see an almost deserted station.

Manchester Central in 1951. Where you have stations you have trains, and where you have trains you have train spotters, like these two little lads with pencils and paper at the end of Platform 5.

Black five-number 44855 on a down freight passes the Goods Warehouse at Heaton Norris in April 1966. These Stanier locomotives were used for both freight and passenger services, and could be found anywhere in the LMS region.

A 1938 photograph of 'E' shop at Gorton Locomotive Works, in Manchester. Here, two A5s, 5030 and 5168 are being constructed in May 1938.

Newton Heath was the big motive power depot to the north of Manchester (26A). Here we see LMS No.11114 undergoing repairs at Newton Heath in July 1933.

LMS No.46115 *Scots Guardsman* leaving Manchester's London Road Station with the 10am express for Euston, London. The photograph was taken on 28 April 1960 and work was just starting on electrification of the station. The overhead wires were for the Guide Bridge and Glossop traffic. *(Photograph: Locofotas)*

A metrolink tram negotiates Mosley Street in the summer of 2001.

A tram descends to the restricted running on the streets of Manchester in 2000. When Manchester's last tram ran on the morning of 10 January 1949, nobody expected to see this form of transport back on the streets of the city. Metrolink arrived in Manchester in 1992 and the city celebrated the return of the tram. The Metrolink system is rapid light railway system that uses two disused railway lines, connected by a route through the streets of the city. When the plans were put forward the Manchester to Bury electric railway line needed modernisation and had old rolling stock, while the Altrincham railway line was also showing its age. Linking the two lines was a great idea, but nonetheless mistakes were made during the project.

Had the new trams been built in England, hundreds of men would have been kept off benefit. The ex-British rail shops at Doncaster and Crewe could have handled the order, but the price of paying unemployment benefit is never taken into account when work is sent abroad to make cost savings. The only parts of the Metrolink network made in England are the electric motors and some of the signalling equipment.

In European cities, all trams have street-level boarding. However, because Metrolink inherited two railway lines, they decided, to save a few bob, to board at platform level. This has resulted in the building of high-level platforms throughout the city, blocking Market Street top and creating an obstacle course in St Peter's Square. The stations Metrolink inherited were old, and the buildings are now too large for their purpose and are falling in to disrepair.

The Metrolink line out to East Manchester should have been completed before the Commonwealth Games, and a connection with the airport will take thousands of cars away from airport parking. Both these projects are currently stalled, as the present operators wait to see whether they will retain their license before releasing funds. This means that the Commonwealth Games stadium will be left with only road connections.

Manchester's first air receiving station, as it was known, was in Trafford Park and was constructed under the supervision of A.V. Roe, founder of the famous aircraft company. Mr Henry G. Melly of Liverpool, grandfather of the gentlemanly and famous George Melly, was an early aviator. He once wrote to Roe to arrange a meeting, and asked for instructions on how to find Trafford Park air strip. Roe replied: 'Fly south from Waterloo until you are over the River Mersey, turn upriver and follow the river the ship canal. When you have gone 25 miles look out for factories and we will put down white sheets where you can land'. Melly found Trafford Park on 7 July 1911 and had lunch with Roe at the Trafford Park Hotel. Melly became the first person to land and take off in Manchester.

Manchester's second airport was on Hough End playing fields, which were leased by Lord Egerton as part of his war effort in 1917. Lord Egerton was himself a keen pilot and held aviation licence No.11. He was the first man to use radio from an aeroplane. There had been an air strip on Cringle playing fields, although it was more a test strip for planes built at the No.2 National Aircraft factory off High Lane, Heaton Chapel. After the war the Air Force continued flying but civil flying did not become a viable proposition. It was not until the mid-1930s that Manchester started to plan a civil airport and settled on Barton as the site of the project. For a time there was a makeshift landing field in Wythenshawe.

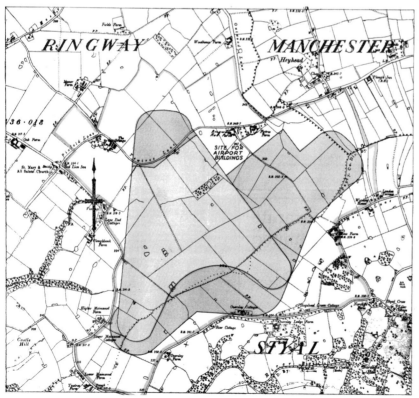

Map dating from 1937 – plans for the new airport.

Chapter Eight

POLICE, FIRE AND AMBULANCE

IN THE Middle Ages, under the system run by the Court Leet of Manchester, there were two constables who dealt with 'bloodsheds, outcries, affrays and rescues'. This situation was preserved until 1839, when a nightwatch constable was added. Later that year work began to establish a police force in Manchester, but it was 1 October 1842 before all the paperwork and by-laws had been put in place and 'bobbies' appeared on Manchester's streets. Until the outbreak of World War Two in 1939, half the cost of running the police force in Manchester was paid for by the government, as long as it was satisfied that the force was being run properly, a fact ascertained by a body of inspectors that visited forces across the country regularly. When the force was first formed, it also carried out the duties of an ambulance service and fire brigade. When Manchester Town Hall opened in 1877 it had a large police station in the court yard, complete with some cells and a charge room that are still there today. Over the last 50 years the force has seen many changes and is now the Greater Manchester Police. Foot patrols and policemen on horseback have returned to some areas of the city and have been warmly welcomed.

A photograph of the Manchester police force of around 1865, tall hats and all.

Manchester Mobile Flying Squad show off the latest form of transport in 1935. The police box behind them stood at Ardwick Green and was a miniature police station, manned by an officer and housing an emergency telephone. Similar boxes were placed across the city, as by the 1930s the police were making cutbacks and closing large old police stations, which had housed policemen and their families. These larger stations were replaced by section houses, each with an office, kitchen and toilet, and the police boxes. Constables were supposed to report to the section house at the end of their beat.

In 1930 the Manchester police owned 55 pedal cycles, and by 1946, when this picture was taken, the number had risen to 73. The cycle officers were not just on patrol duty, they acted as despatch riders, taking messages, and as first aiders, rushing off to the scene of accidents or fires.

Manchester has always had a strong section of mounted police, and in the 1930s when this picture was taken they had their work cut out controlling not only large football crowds, but also by the unemployed and other demonstrations.

The new six-storey police station on South Street and Bootle Street, just after it was completed in 1937. It looks dark because the picture was taken at night to demonstrate how good the gas floodlighting was. The foundation stone was laid on 6 September 1934, and the building opened on 16 July 1937.

Modernisation hits traffic duty in Manchester. An official demonstrates the first set of traffic lights in the city. They were manually controlled by the police officer on duty, but just one officer could control a busy junction, whereas before it had taken two or even three.

Fire appliances lined up for inspection at London Road Fire Station, *c.*1928. Note the children on the balcony watching the proceedings. When the fire station opened in 1906, it contained 47 large flats for families on the first floor, and rooms for 51 single men higher up. At one time it was the largest in the north of England.

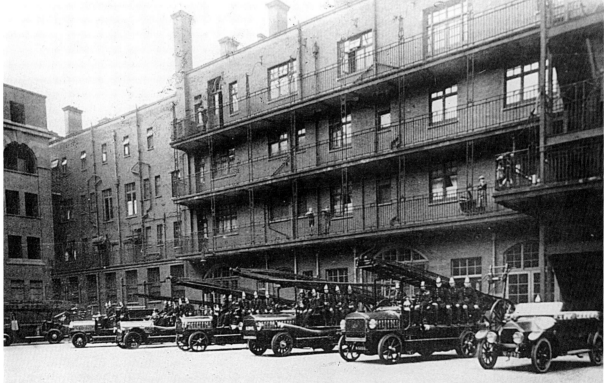

The fire brigade, with help from the police, tackle a large fire in central Manchester in 1938.

When the Americans joined World War One in 1916, aircraft were sent over from the US. They arrived by ship at Salford Docks and were then taken to Failsworth to be put together. This is the American Aircraft Acceptance Park at Failsworth in 1919, just after the end of the war.

Many wounded and shell-shocked war victims came to the Manchester area to recuperate during World War One. Many of the cottage hospitals on the city's outskirts were turned into military hospitals. This postcard shows the war wounded, complete with their uniform caps (including an ANZAC soldier), resting at the YMCA in Piccadilly, Manchester.

Manchester Fire Brigade with a horse-drawn appliance from around 1880. Manchester's first fire station was in Town Yard, which stood where the town hall is today.

The Cenotaph in St Peter's Square, Manchester, as it appeared in 1926. The 'Monument to the Fallen of the Great War' was designed by Sir Edward Lutyens in 1920, and is a Grade II* listed monument.

On 15 June 1996 Manchester City Centre was devastated by an IRA bomb. A Northern Ireland terrorist decided to cause mayhem in a city that had a large, peaceful Irish community. It was the biggest bomb ever detonated on the English mainland, calculated to cause death and destruction. A friend of mine was in Manchester at the Museum of Science & Industry on the day of the explosion and felt the blast. He was on the platform of the station, and said that the plate glass behind him bent with the force. Luckily it was studded with rubber buffers. He took a picture only seconds after the blast and this is that photograph, looking over Granada into the city centre.

Chapter Nine

PEOPLE AND PLACES

THERE WAS a saying that was popular 150 years ago: Liverpool produced gentlemen, Lancashire brought up lads, but Manchester bred men. This summed up the social feeling of the time. Manchester can claim many famous sons and daughters and even more adopted offspring: some are household names, but more have faded into the shadows as their lives and achievements are consigned to history. John Dalton and James Joule were giants in the history of physics, and are remembered in statues and a street name. Joule, of course, gave his name to a unit of energy. Joseph Whitworth was a great man who made his name and his money by putting a thread on a nail and calling it a screw. He made armaments, but left Manchester with a street and an art gallery, and much more. Ernest and Sheena Simon were shining angels of their time and as well as working for the ordinary Mancunian, gave Wythenshawe Park to the people. Alfred Darbyshire was a genius who saved thousands of lives. Harrison Ainsworth was one of England's greatest writers and gave Charles Dickens his first break. These are just a few of the people that Manchester has produced: their stories and those of other important personages could easily fill the pages of a whole book.

A view of the stall at the top of Shude Hill, Manchester in the area that had once been the 'Hen Market'. Tony's record stall is offering records at 3s, down to 1s for a 78rpm. Those 78s had to be carried very carefully, as they were easily cracked and broken. Norton's radio shop is next door, nearer to the camera, with Allan's bookstall outside it. The view dates from the late 1950s.

A rare view of the Hen Market when it really did sell hens. The cages can be seen on the right. Racing pigeons, rabbits and bantam hens were also on sale.

The top market at Smithfield was covered in and was strictly wholesale. Here is that market just before World War Two. Fred Turner Ltd is on the lorry, and John Rose's stall is in the centre of the picture. In around 1980 the market moved further out of town. Smithfield Market was one of the traditional areas of Manchester, where farmers and wholesalers would sell fresh produce to the people of the town. On Saturday, the produce got cheaper as the day wore on, and after teatime poorer Mancunians would go to pick up the bargains as traders wanted to sell up and get home. Reading older biographies, you hear of families so poor they would pick through the market rubbish to find something to put in the 'tater ash' for their next meal.

The Bridgewater Hall on Lower Mosley Street, seen from the steps of the G-Mex. It seems odd that the hall should have been named the Bridgewater Hall when in fact it stands on a branch of the Rochdale Canal. The only connection it has with the Bridgewater name is that the street at the rear of the hall is Great Bridgewater Street, but the public do not enter or leave the building from that side. Perhaps they would have been better naming it the Barbirolli Hall. A bust of Barbirolli has now been placed outside the hall. *Inset*: Barbirolli: a man passionate about music and Manchester.

All the recent statues in Manchester put together cost less than the 'pebble'. This is the city's contribution to the Bridgewater Hall. A Japanese artist was commissioned to create it, and the city flew him and his family to Manchester while he did the work. The cost of protecting it from graffiti is considerable.

Quay Street public baths and wash house, on the corner of Back Quay Street, Manchester, 1916. There had been private wash-houses and baths since 1856, but the Manchester Corporation entered the business on 29 September 1877, taking over the Manchester & Salford Laundry Co. premises at Leaf Street and Mayfield (Ardwick). At the beginning of 1936, the Corporation had many establishments, including 24 public baths and 20 washhouses, as well as a central laundry which opened in February 1931.

The swimming baths and baths for washing, like those we now have in our homes, were used by those who had no bath in their houses. Families would go down to the wash baths, where the father might book a three-halfpenny bath. The whole family might take turns in the same water, baby going last. There were also vapour baths and Turkish baths in some of the establishments.

The Midland Hotel has occupied an important place in Manchester society. It was here in the winter garden that Henry Royce and Charles Rolls had their meeting and decided to go into partnership. Most of the stars that appeared at the Palace Theatre in the 1950s and 1960s stayed here, including Frank Sinatra, Danny Kaye and Bing Crosby. Last year it was still frequented by George Best and Jackie Stewart, so it is still a favourite haunt among celebrities.

'Wisdom is the principle thing, therefore get wisdom' runs one of the mottos around the ceiling of the Great Hall of Manchester's Central Library, pictured here just after it opened in 1934. The hall was light and spacious at the time, but modern demands have made it a much more crowded place today.

One of the character pubs of Manchester was Tommy Duck's, which stood on East Street just off Oxford Street and Lower Mosley Street. It was a favourite haunt of actors and theatre people for many years, then in the 1960s the publican developed a habit of collecting ladies underwear to glue or hang on the ceiling. It was wiped out overnight, just as a fight to preserve it was getting under way. Greenall Whitley were fined £7,000 for pulling it down without waiting for the outcome of the inquiry, but it was too late. The most plausible explanation for the original name of the pub runs that the sign writer was promised a drink for every letter he painted on the large signboard outside the public house. By the time he got halfway through Duckworth he had had enough to drink and went home and Tommy Duck's got its name.

The Chinese Arch in Faulkner Street, Manchester. Built in the heart of the Chinese community, it adds colour and excitement to the area.

An unusual Manchester monument. John Noel Nichols started work as a stockbroker's clerk, but his hobby and interest was herbs. He set up as a herbalist in Granby Row, Manchester, and started mixing 'medicines'. He mixed his first 'Vim-tonic' in 1908 and it was an immediate success. The Temperance movement liked it and Vimto became a household name. The company decided to erect a monument on the site of that first warehouse/factory and commissioned sculptress Kerry Morrison to produce it.

A pub of character that is now lost is the Crown and Kettle at New Cross, the corner of Great Ancoats Street and Oldham Road. This building started life as a magistrates court then became a public house. It has been closed and empty now for over 10 years. It seems to be owned by The Express Group of Newspapers, or at least whoever owns the Express building. It was going to be flats and accommodation for newspaper executives staying in Manchester, but at present all plans seem to be on hold. The people outside the pub are GMR (BBC radio) listeners, on a history evening walk, led by the author. The landlord in the 1930s bought carriages from the underneath of one of the great airships of the day, and lined the bar and walls with the fine wood panelling. *Below:* one of the bars with the wood from the airship.

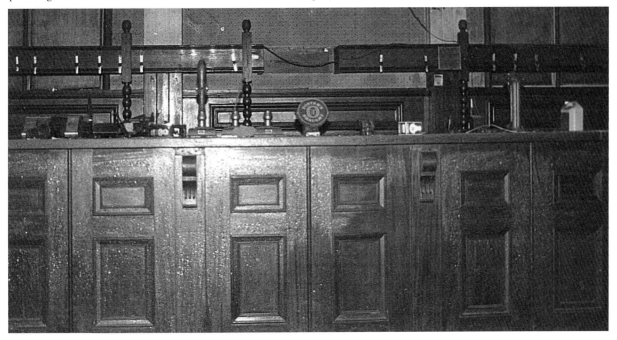

In 1993 and 1994 I was on local radio more or less every week. This enabled me to build up a following and together with local radio personality, Fred Fielder, we turned out every Monday night for a history walk round a different part of Manchester. Twenty turned up for the first one and two years later 200 turned up for the last one. It was hard work, but very enjoyable. On the last walk the police turned up and warned us about crossing the road *en masse* and holding up traffic. Happy Days!

We went everywhere and saw a lot of history. We rode the trams in Heaton Park, visited the Bus Museum, walked round Castlefield and attended classes in the Ragged School complete with slates for doing sums on. Here Fred and the author pose for a photograph for the *Manchester Evening News*.

One of the trips included a tour of the Town Hall, and an ascent of the tower to see the bells. Here I am with David Peart, one of the listeners, counting the number of bells hanging in the tower.

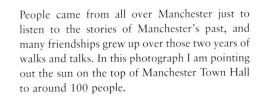

People came from all over Manchester just to listen to the stories of Manchester's past, and many friendships grew up over those two years of walks and talks. In this photograph I am pointing out the sun on the top of Manchester Town Hall to around 100 people.

Sometimes we even took the bus and off we went around Manchester to explore its historic nooks and crannies. This is one such party after an enjoyable day out. Fred Fielder is on the left at the back, complete with cap.

Chapter Ten

THE CITY AT LEISURE

'WORK HARD, and play hard' seems to have been Manchester's motto. Maybe among the working classes, boozing would be counted as a leisure activity, but then drink helped block out the horror of back-to-back tenements, and the terrible working conditions that many had to endure.

Mancunians were always willing to try a new form of relaxation, and were the first in the north to take up golf. They were also among the first to take up horse racing, pigeon racing and football. Even in the days of the cruel sports of bull-baiting and cock-fighting, a lot of it went on in the city before spreading to the rest of Lancashire and Cheshire. A hundred and fifty years ago, there was reference to 'cat fighting' or 'purring', and 'up and down' fighting. Women, sometimes naked to the waist, would stick metal and glass into their hobnail boots and fight each other, kicking and pulling hair. Men paid sixpence to watch this spectacle in the back room of a pub. Times were hard then, and the working man wanted to forget his hum-drum life.

Belle Vue Gardens were started in 1836 by John Jennison. He had run an inn in the Stockport area and had made it popular by introducing cages of small animals in the garden. He saved his profits and bought the site at Belle Vue. It was only by very hard work and some luck that the gardens survived the first few years as growth was slow. The introduction of a fun fair to the Zoological Gardens was a big step forward. John Jennison died on 20 September 1869 aged 80, by which time the zoo had become well established. It was managed by his sons.

'All the nice girls love a sailor' and here are a party enjoying a ride on the 'Bobs' at Belle Vue in around 1946.

Another busy day at Belle Vue. It really was a Mecca of entertainment and on Bank Holidays and summer weekends trains would pull into Belle Vue Station from towns all over Lancashire and Cheshire. Judging by the dress styles, and the many uniforms, the photograph probably dates from around 1945.

After a 1958 fire in the Belle Vue ballroom a new Elizabethan-style ballroom was opened. In the entrance a 'Hall of Fame' was begun, where celebrities left their hand and footprints in concrete. Gracie Fields was first, followed by such luminaries as Sir John Barbirolli, Bing Crosby, Bob Hope, Pele and Jimmy Clitheroe.

The Floral Clock and the monkey cage and, behind the monkey mountain, a new experimental concrete structure, as seen in around 1955. Belle Vue would always try something different. Firework displays, brass band contests, balloon flights, wrestling, greyhound racing and 10-pin bowling were all at Belle Vue long before they became commonplace elsewhere.

An aerial photograph of the Belle Vue Pleasure Gardens in 1949. The speedway track is on the very left and the lake and the Lake Hotel are in the centre. The King's Hall and tea rooms are just above the lake and the two separate big dippers can be seen to the right.

All the fun of the fair: Belle Vue in the 1950s. There were two big fires at the complex. In January 1958 the ballroom burnt down completely. Judy, the lioness, panicked and had to be shot. In October 1963 the Fun House burnt down.

The zoo closed and the animals were sold off as interest waned in the late 1970s. Then the fair closed. There was a little protest but not enough to change the view of Manchester Council, which had by then approved plans for building houses on the site.

The Palace Theatre, Manchester, with its ornate and elaborate top, as it appeared in 1911. Even before it opened in 1891 the Palace Theatre was the centre of controversy. The Temperance Movement vigorously opposed a drinks license being granted to the new theatre, and it opened and ran for some time 'dry'. Alfred Darbyshire, the architect, fell out with the publicans who had premises near the theatre construction site. They sued him for using dynamite and making too much noise during the construction, and for breaking glasses and bottles. He in turn sued them for enticing workmen to drink too much so they were not able to work. In 1913 the theatre was almost completely rebuilt and the cupolas on the roof were removed as the whole outside became more streamlined. It closed in 1978 but was saved by local entrepreneur Raymond Slater and reopened as a Trust in 1981.

Another theatre which played a large part in entertaining Manchester was the Empire at Ardwick Green. All signs of it have now gone completely, and we only have the Apollo Theatre on the opposite corner.

The Ardwick Green Empire opened as a Vaudeville theatre (seats 3d, 4d and 6d) in 1904. The photograph shows an open-topped tram passing the theatre, heading back to Manchester in around 1906. In 1935 it changed its name to the New Manchester Hippodrome, after the original Hippodrome on Oxford Street closed down. It finally closed in 1961 and plans for a bowling alley or bingo hall were put forward. The theatre burnt down in February 1964 and by autumn 1964 all trace of it had gone.

SAILOR BEWARE!

—

CHARACTERS *in order of their appearance:*

Edie Hornett	MARION WILSON
Emma Hornett	.. TESSIE O'SHEA
Mrs. Lack	.. NATALIE KENT
Henry Hornett	.. CYRIL SMITH
Albert Tufnell, A.B.	GODFREY JAMES
Carnoustie Bligh, A.B.	ANDREW DOWNIE
Daphne Pink	CHERRY CREST
Shirley Hornett	JENNIFER SCHOOLING
The Rev. Oliver Purefoy	ALAN ROLFE

—

Produced by MELVILLE GILLAM

Settings by MICHAEL EVE

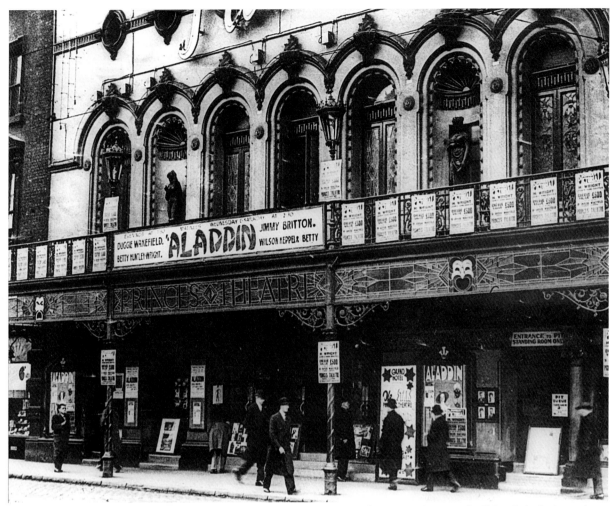

The Prince's Theatre, Oxford Street, Manchester, as it was in 1936. The pantomimes at the Prince's had always been special and that year it was *Aladdin*. Among the acts taking part were Wilson, Kepple and Betty, the sand dancers. The theatre opened in 1864 but by the time of this photograph it was struggling against the new super cinemas. It was the first theatre with tip-up seats, and also started the system of 'early doors', where those paying top prices could go in early and avoid the queues. Its closed in April 1940 and was pulled down almost immediately. There were plans to build a large cinema on the site but the Blitz put paid to that. Eventually Peter House was built on the corner of Lower Mosley Street and Peter Street.

The Manchester Races were popular for over 300 years, although they were in fact held in Salford. The first recorded horse-racing around here took place on Kersal Moor, Salford, on 2 May 1687, but we know that horse racing had taken place here even before that. A challenge between two gentlemen on horseback was known as a 'match', and would be run in heats of up to three miles at a time. This was how horse-racing was conducted centuries ago, with one 'match' or 'contest' taking all day. Between the rounds as the horses rested there would be cock-fighting, eating and drinking and other amusements. On Kersal Moor they held 'smock races', when scantily-clad ladies and nearly or completely naked men would race round and over the moor for a new smock or shirt. These were reported in the diary of Oliver Heywood from September 1681.

Horse-racing was officially held on Kersal Moor until 1847, when it moved to Castle Irwell. St Paul's Church was built on some of the racecourse land at Kersal Moor and a graveyard was opened where the stands used to be. Years later the skeleton of a horse, complete with saddle and bridle, was found, but the story behind it is a mystery.

In 1827 the Earl of Wilton laid out a racecourse at his home in Heaton Park and held races there. They were supposed to be just for his friends and the servants, but thousands would turn up to watch.

The following year he gave orders that no one was to be admitted on foot, so the people of Manchester turned up on milk carts, farm carts and even perambulators. The races were transferred to Lord Derby's estate in Liverpool after the Wilton's married into the Stanley family.

A view looking over the course toward the stands in around 1950. At first races only took place at New Year, then a November meet was added and by 1910 the annual Manchester Whit Holiday was also on the racing calendar. The Manchester November Handicap was the last major flat race of the year. During World War Two the St Leger was run in Salford, the only time Manchester has hosted a 'classic'.

Looking over the Castle Irwell site toward Manchester. Everything was going well in 1960 and racing was popular. Then the directors were offered a lot of money for the land, which was wanted to build a housing estate on. They accepted, and horse-racing in Manchester finished after the three-day November meeting in 1963.

The Manchester races were a busy time for a lot of people. Hotels were full, taxis were busy and cafés and restaurants overflowed. There was overtime for the police, stable hands were hired for the week, and of course, the bookies did a roaring trade. There were no betting shops in those days, at least no official ones. Slipping on a bet in a pub or nipping down an alley to put a bet on was how most people gambled.

Parks have played a big part in Manchester recreation. During World War Two people had 'stay at home' holidays, and special events were put on in Whitworth and other parks. This is Whitworth Park, Manchester, with the King Edward VII statue and the Whitworth Art Gallery behind it. The gallery and park were gifts from the estate of Sir Joseph Whitworth, who died in 1887. The gallery, which has a wonderful collection of Victorian wallpapers, opened in 1889, but it took a few years to lay out the park and that opened in 1904. The statue was a gift from James Gresham, and cost over £5,000. Inset: Children's dancing lessons held in the open air at Crowcroft Park in 1928. Maybe they were getting ready to move on to the Ritz.

Whitworth Park at its very best, seen in around 1925. This 18-acre park was the nearest to the city centre of the larger parks, and was very popular. In the very centre of the postcard is another statue. This is a terracotta group entitled 'Christ and the Little Children' and was a gift from Robert Dunkinfield Darbyshire, who had been one of the overseers of the Whitworth Estate and put a lot of effort into the development of Whitworth Park.

Swimming was always a popular recreation, and between the wars Manchester had 24 public baths. Here we see the main pool of one of the largest, Victoria Baths, during a Sunday morning mixed bathing session in 1929. Mixed bathing was allowed two days a week at the Victoria Baths, though for just half a day in most other baths. It had been like that since 1919, when official mixed bathing was allowed by the city council. The Victoria Baths also had Turkish baths, vapour baths and Russian baths.

During the winter (November to March) the baths that had two pools would convert one of them to a public hall. Here we see a pool at Victoria Baths in its winter garb: it was used as a reception room for weddings and 21st birthdays. The baths at Chorlton, Harpurhey, Levenshulme and Broadway also had winter public halls. It was strange for any band playing in these rooms, as the large empty space beneath the stage and dancers played havoc with the sound, and caused feedback on microphone systems.

Victoria Baths, Victoria Park, Manchester. Built in 1905 and opened in 1906, the baths closed around 20 years ago. The lovely building has since been used for youth schemes and council department offices, and the present scheme is to use it to house craft shops.

Manchester people liked their holidays, and fair days and Whitsuntide were particularly popular for a short break at the seaside. Here we see solid-tyred coaches loading up for Blackpool at Whitsun, in around 1925.

ALL MANCHESTER'S GOING

REAL ICE SKATING

The Exhilarating "Skate-way" to Health

OPEN TO THE PUBLIC

Mondays, Wednesdays and Saturdays. (3 Sessions)

ALSO TUESDAY AND FRIDAY MORNINGS, AND THURSDAY EVENINGS

CLUBS. TUESDAYS and FRIDAYS—AFTERNOON and EVENING
Also Sunday (Private Club). Visitors to Tuesday & Friday Evening Clubs 3/6

CURLING • ICE HOCKEY • EXHIBITIONS

BRITAIN'S FIRST and
MANCHESTER'S ONLY ICE RINK

ICE PALACE

DERBY ST., CHEETHAM, MANCHESTER

BERTRAM E. WAKE, Sec. Manager
WRITE FOR BOOKLET—POST FREE. Phone : BLA 9698

RESTAURANT, CAFE, DRESSING ROOMS, BATHROOMS, LOUNGES and all the appointments of a First Class Club. Extensive New Club Rooms and Skate Locker Room. EXPERT TUITION— STAFF OF FAMOUS SKATING STARS

Manchester once boasted a large ice rink, in Derby Street, just off Cheetham Hill Road, quite near the city centre. It was the first purpose-built ice rink in Britain, others being only outdoor frozen ponds. Other places followed Manchester but they converted to roller-skating rinks in the summer. The Ice Palace in Manchester was a luxurious and classy place. In *Shabby Tiger* by Howard Spring, one of the main characters goes to the ice rink and it is described in detail. During World War One the rink was turned into an aircraft factory and planes were brought there to be repaired and overhauled. They landed at Alexandra Park, then with their wings taken off they were pulled through the streets, up to three at a time, by milk floats. The building today is a cool storage area for a dairy firm. There were plans in the late sixties and early seventies for a national ice rink to be built where the Bridgewater Hall is today, but the plans were shelved because of a lack of government interest.

Chapter Eleven

TRAFFORD PARK AND THE MANCHESTER SHIP CANAL CO.

T HE TRAFFORD family who have now given their name to the Metropolitan Borough Council, were given the land in this area by King Canute and pre-date the Norman Conquest. In fact a Trafford fought on the side of Harold at the Battle of Hastings. They soon changed sides, and to show their new allegiance became the de Traffords. They originally lived at Trafford Bar, but moved when the Bridgewater Canal was built in 1765 and disturbed their quiet life. They moved into what had been their country estate and weekend retreat, Trafford Park. The house they left behind became Old Trafford Hall, and later Old Trafford, and so a famous name was born.

The family was rich and powerful and managed to stay on friendly terms with whoever was in power in England. In the 15th century a de Trafford was granted a license to turn base metal into gold and produce an elixir to make one younger.

It was the building of the Manchester Ship Canal which finally drove the de Traffords out of the area. The 25th Lord de Trafford had fought tooth and nail against the building of the canal, but when he died his son decided to move away. He owned large areas of the Midlands, which had been given to his father by the Earl of Shrewsbury on his marriage to the earl's sister, Annette de Talbot. Trentham Hall and gardens was one of his wedding presents. The estate was offered to the Manchester Corporation for £260,000, which although it feigned interest, seemed determined not to conclude the sale. Eventually E.T. Hooley bought the estate and put ship canal manager Marshall Stevens in charge of developing it. The result was Trafford Park, the world's first industrial park. From nothing he created a whole village of workers to supply the incoming factories with willing labour.

When the Trafford Park Development Co. first started the plans passed to them by owner E.T. Hooley were very different from how things turned out. Hooley ended up in jail for fraud and control passed to Barings Bank and Lord Ashburton. The original idea was for half of the estate to be industrial (there were already saw mills at Trafford Wharf), and half to be leisure. The plans included a golf course, which was created; a cycle track and velodrome, and horse-racing. Buffalo Bill's American Circus was a great attraction in the park in the early 1900s.

Trafford Hall, seen in 1905 when it was the club house for the Manchester Golf Co. The front was built when the family moved here to make it their main residence in around 1770, but parts of the hall dated back to 150 years before that.

Westinghouse Road runs across the bottom of this picture and the head office (the big house) of British Westinghouse Corporation is visible at the bottom left. Because Marshall Stevens had American connections he was able to persuade Henry Ford and George Westinghouse to set up in Trafford Park.

Barton Power Station, seen from the air in the mid-1920s. The Ship Canal is at the top of the picture, and the Bridgewater Canal also runs across the photograph. The power station was built at Barton because coal could easily be delivered from the Worsley mines further down the canal.

Marshall Stevens' plans were almost faultless. Houses were created for the workers right next to the factories; and all the necessary amenities were provided for them. Factory owners welcomed this ready-made workforce. Here we see Second Street, in the park, which was unusual in that the houses had gardens. On Fourth Avenue there were villas, large four-bedroom houses where the police sergeant, the doctor and other officials lived.

The trams that ran into Trafford Park were, in the early years, Manchester ones. Salford Corporation Transport came along a little later. To simplify matters the lines were laid out in a one-way system. At starting and finishing time there could be as many as 30 trams full of workers coming and going. Ladies were let out five minutes early at Westinghouse to avoid the crush. Here we see two trams on Third Avenue waiting for the journey home, in around 1910. Trafford Park has a good heritage centre on Third Avenue. It is housed in what was the Catholic school of St Antony's and is well worth a visit.

Westinghouse was taken over by the Metropolitan Carriage Company, which was later amalgamated with Vickers Electrical to become Metro-Vicks. This view is of clocking-off time at Metro-Vicks in the early 1950s.

Eleventh Street, Trafford Park, in 1911. This was where the American Ford workers were housed when they arrived in Britain in 1904. Some just stayed for 12 months to train the English workers, but some were integrated into the park life and stayed.

Trafford Park did develop some leisure interests. Manchester United Football Club moved into the park in 1910. The first game was against old rivals Liverpool, on 19 February, which they lost 3–4. This 1934 view looks from above Kings Road, Stretford, toward Trafford Park. The Lancashire County Cricket Ground, Old Trafford, is nearest the camera, in the left-hand corner. Stretford Town Hall, still under construction is next, with the White City greyhound track to the right of it. Behind that is the Manchester United ground, Old Trafford.

As Trafford Park developed, the industries became more diverse. This photograph shows the Jacobs Cream Cracker factory in 1910. Kilverts Lard was another food-related industry in the park.

A view of the No.6 dock at Salford, *c.*1930. When plans were first laid to build docks in the Manchester area, Ordsall was really the only open area large enough to accommodate them. Only the top half of No.1 dock is actually inside the Manchester boundary.

A wartime scene of barges unloading grain from a convoy ship which has braved the Atlantic in its grey camouflage paint. *(Photograph: Manchester Ship Canal Co.)*

View in No. 9 Dock, Manchester.

PORT OF MANCHESTER

The Port for the Industrial North and Midlands

UNRIVALLED FACILITIES FOR QUICK DISCHARGE AND DISPATCH OF CARGO

EXTENSIVE SHEDS, WAREHOUSES AND OPEN STORAGE ACCOMMODATION

RAIL CONNECTION BETWEEN SHIPSIDE AND ALL TRUNK RAILWAY SYSTEMS

THROUGH RAILWAY RATES INCLUSIVE OF SHIP CANAL TOLLS QUOTED

COAL AND OIL BUNKERING   GRAVING DOCKS AND PONTOONS

::   REFRIGERATED CHAMBERS   ::
TWO 40,000 TON GRAIN ELEVATORS
OVER 115 MILLION GALLONS OIL TANKAGE

Sites for Factories, Works and Depots with deep-water frontage and rail, road and inland navigation connections

For all particulars concerning the Port apply to the—

MANCHESTER SHIP CANAL COMPANY
::   DOCK OFFICE, MANCHESTER   ::

A very full No.8 dock, showing the 60-ton floating crane unloading the Norwegian ship *Brunyard* in September 1976. The sheds behind the ship are today the site of the Lowry Centre. *(Photograph: E. Gray)*

The No.6 dock seen in December 1973. The SS *Bratha Fisher* is on the left and *Clan Maclay* is on the right. Containerisation had just begun. Ordsall's high rise flats are in the middle of the background. *(Photograph: E. Gray)*

The swing bridge at the bottom of Trafford Road, seen in 1990 just before the road was widened and Trafford Road was made into a dual carriageway.

Chapter Twelve

MANCHESTER TODAY

WALKING around Manchester today, there is a lot of building going on. There is hardly a main street in town where rebuilding work is not going on. Is it all just for the Commonwealth Games in 2002, or is Manchester really transforming itself for the new millennium? Can Manchester attract the numbers of people required to make all this progress profitable? That remains to be seen.

The open area at the Castlefield Basin, one of the successes of Manchester's rejuvenation.

Another success for the city, turning the old dilapidated City Hall into the Air and Space Hall of the Manchester Museum of Science & Industry.

The whole of the Liverpool Road area has been modernised and transformed. Even the old Sunday School has a new lease of life as offices.

When the *Daily Mirror* moved out to Trafford Park Thompson House stood empty until being sold in the mid-1990s. Here we see the view from Fennel Street in 1998 as the Printworks advertised all that was to come.

Thomson House, gutted with only the outside walls standing. The Swan with Two Necks, which stood next door, closed when it lost 4,000 print customers.

The Corn Exchange Building, photographed in 1995 just before its metamorphosis into the Triangle.

There was a lot of work to be done on the Corn Exchange, and Fennel Street was closed off to complete that work. This view looks down Fennel Street while the construction was in progress.

Crown Square, Manchester, 1990. It has always has been a windswept and unfriendly place. At the moment it is awaiting demolition, and the area will be completely revamped.

Another building whose days are numbered – Northcliffe House, Deansgate. It was built in 1904 and the tower was added in the late 1920s. The plans are for a massive hotel to rise on this spot.

The Lowry Centre at Salford Quays opened in 2000, as a millennium project. Here it is under construction in 1999.

Manchester has plenty of new bars and restaurants. Barca, seen here on a sunny day in 2000, is one of the most successful and attracts many of Manchester's celebrities.

Baguley Hall, Wythenshawe, 2000. The oldest building in Manchester is now in the hands of English Heritage. Part of the building was constructed in the 14th century, and it has a mediaeval north wing and a south part built in around 1690. For many years it was a farmhouse and a family home, and this is why it was never modernised. Heaton Hall, and Wythenshawe Hall, seem to be looked after very well in council hands, but the story of Baguley Hall is not a happy one. Nobody seems to want to buy the property and its future looks bleak. *Above* we see the front of the hall from Old Hall Lane, and *below* we see the back of the hall, with its ancient wooden frame and doorway.

The Castlefield Basin and the new bridge that spans the very end of the Bridgewater Canal. Though there has been a lot of development in this area, it still a quiet backwater near the city centre.

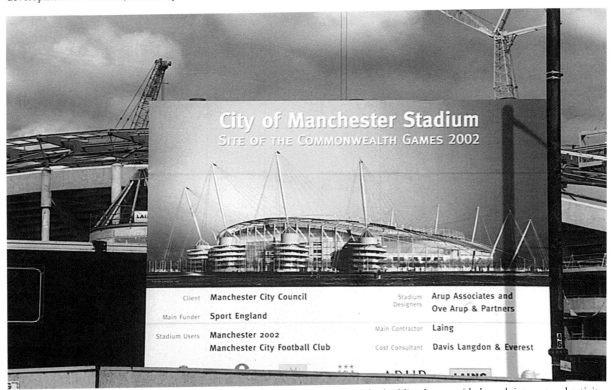

Manchester is hosting the 2002 Commonwealth Games, and the building and rebuilding has provided much interest and activity.

The Eastlands Stadium is being constructed for the Commonwealth Games in 2002. This is what the view was like in 1994, before all the construction work started. It was formerly the site of the works of Richard Johnson and Nephew, wire manufacturers, which had been closing down over the years. The firm moved to Ambergate, near Eyam in Derbyshire.

Construction work on the Eastlands Stadium, well under way in May 2001. It will all be ready for July 2002 and the opening ceremony. Manchester City Football club are set to take it over after the Commonwealth Games and will move there from their Maine Road ground.